THE BATTLE
FOR THE
RAILWAYS
1940–41

THE BATTLE FOR THE RAILWAYS 1940–41

HOW BRITAIN'S RAIL STAFF DEFIED THE LUFTWAFFE

MATTHEW RICHARDSON

First published in Great Britain in 2025 by
Pen and Sword Transport
An imprint of
Pen & Sword Books Ltd.
Yorkshire - Philadelphia

ISBN 978 1 03610 744 4

A CIP catalogue record for this book is available from the British Library.

Typeset in 11.5/15 pt Palatino
Typeset by SJmagic DESIGN SERVICES, India.
Printed and bound in the UK by CPI Group (UK) Ltd.

The Publisher's authorised representative in the EU for product safety is Authorised Rep Compliance Ltd., Ground Floor, 71 Lower Baggot Street, Dublin D02 P593, Ireland. www.arccompliance.com

For a complete list of Pen & Sword titles please contact

PEN & SWORD BOOKS LIMITED
George House, Units 12 & 13, Beevor Street, Off Pontefract Road,
Barnsley, S71 1HN, UK
E-mail: enquiries@pen-and-sword.co.uk
Website: www.pen-and-sword.co.uk

or

PEN AND SWORD BOOKS
1950 Lawrence Rd, Havertown, PA 19083, USA
E-mail: uspen-and-sword@casematepublishers.com
Website: www.penandswordbooks.com

CONTENTS

ACKNOWLEDGEMENTS

In any book such as this, the author will of course have many people to thank for their assistance in providing material. I would like to especially mention in this regard Mrs Ivy M. Armitage who entrusted material relating to her late husband Len to my care. Likewise, Mrs Margaret Bowden kindly loaned photographs relating to her father. The family of Mrs Gladys Wilber loaned photographs, and shared memories of her.

Dai Jenkins and Dafydd Roberts helped with specific requests for information, for which I am enormously grateful. Any error of fact or interpretation is my own.

I must pay tribute to my own forebears as my own family archive was the nucleus of the idea for this book. My own great uncle, Victor Green was a driver with London Midland Scottish throughout the war years, retiring in 1967. Ever modest, he would not voluntarily discuss his experiences and sadly he died before I was old enough to really question him about them.

Long experience as a writer has taught me that it is lamentable easy to cause offence by omission. In this book, space has not permitted me to mention every individual who performed bravely or who was decorated during these difficult times. The absence of an individual herein in no way diminishes their actions, or implies that they were somehow less worthy.

Matthew Richardson
Douglas, Isle of Man, 2025

INTRODUCTION

In 1939, Britain possessed the most concentrated and intricate railway system in the world. With the growing likelihood of the outbreak of war, this network passed into government control on 1 September 1939. In this unfolding conflict, Britain's railways would be of vital importance, both in defence and attack. Many people today are aware of the impact of the Blitz in 1940–1941, when Germany's Luftwaffe sought to terrorise the British people into submission through bombing of civilian targets. Few however are aware of the simultaneous Battle for the Railways – the determined efforts by the Luftwaffe to cripple the nation's rail network – and the Herculean efforts of the railway personnel to keep the system running in spite of the difficulties. This phase of the Second World War is an interesting one, for in retrospect it is possible to see at as a period when, prior to the entry of the United States into the war and in the lead up to the invasion of the Soviet Union, Adolf Hitler's focus was upon subduing Great Britain, his last adversary in the west, and forcing her to the negotiating table. His primary tactic was air assault, and in the event the Luftwaffe was not successful in this, partly because their attacks were sporadic and not strategically targeted, but mainly due to the often unseen efforts of the railway staff in keeping the network going. This is the story of those critical, but now largely forgotten months on the Home Front in the Second World War, and of the men and women who endured so much in order to keep this vital industry running.

Chapter One

LONDON MIDLAND SCOTTISH AT WAR

In its day the biggest railway company in Britain, London Midland Scottish (LMS) had been formed by the Grouping Act which brought into existence the 'Big Four' railway companies. This act, introduced in the wake of the First World War, had swept away Britain's myriad of minor rail companies. Besides being the world's largest transport organisation at the time, the company was also the largest commercial enterprise in the British Empire and the United Kingdom's second largest employer, after the Post Office. LMS operated services in and around London, the Midlands, the North West of England, Mid- and North Wales, and Scotland. The company also operated a separate network of lines in Northern Ireland. The principal north-south routes on which its trains ran were the West Coast Main Line and the Midland Main Line, which had been the main arteries of its two largest constituent companies, London and North Western Railway and Midland Railway respectively. In 1938, the LMS operated some 6,870 miles (11,056km) of railway (excluding its lines in Northern Ireland).

The Spanish Civil War in the late 1930s had clearly demonstrated the effectiveness of and destruction brought about by the bombing of civilian targets. As war with Germany loomed ever larger, few could be in any doubt that such bombing of domestic targets would play a significant part in this conflict as well. As early as 1938 the LMS had drawn up emergency plans for

German military intelligence had made a careful study of primary targets in Britain. This is the Stafford-Derrington road bridge, over the LMS line at Stafford Junction. (Public Domain)

the protection of its staff. These covered such topics as air raid organisation, warning systems, lighting restrictions, protective clothing and decontamination squads in case poison gas should be used. It was also realised that in order to deal with large scale damage such as the bombing of a major station, significant stocks of specialised material and equipment should be stored at convenient centres. This consisted of permanent way sections, timber, and steel joists as well as cranes, welding and cutting equipment. Major engineering work was also undertaken to try to increase the resilience of the network by adding extra lines to some stretches and to reduce the number of potential choke points. For example, to the north of Carlisle where the main line from England to Scotland crossed the River Eden, a new bridge was built next to the existing structure to carry two extra lines. This would allow either to carry all traffic if the other was damaged by enemy action.

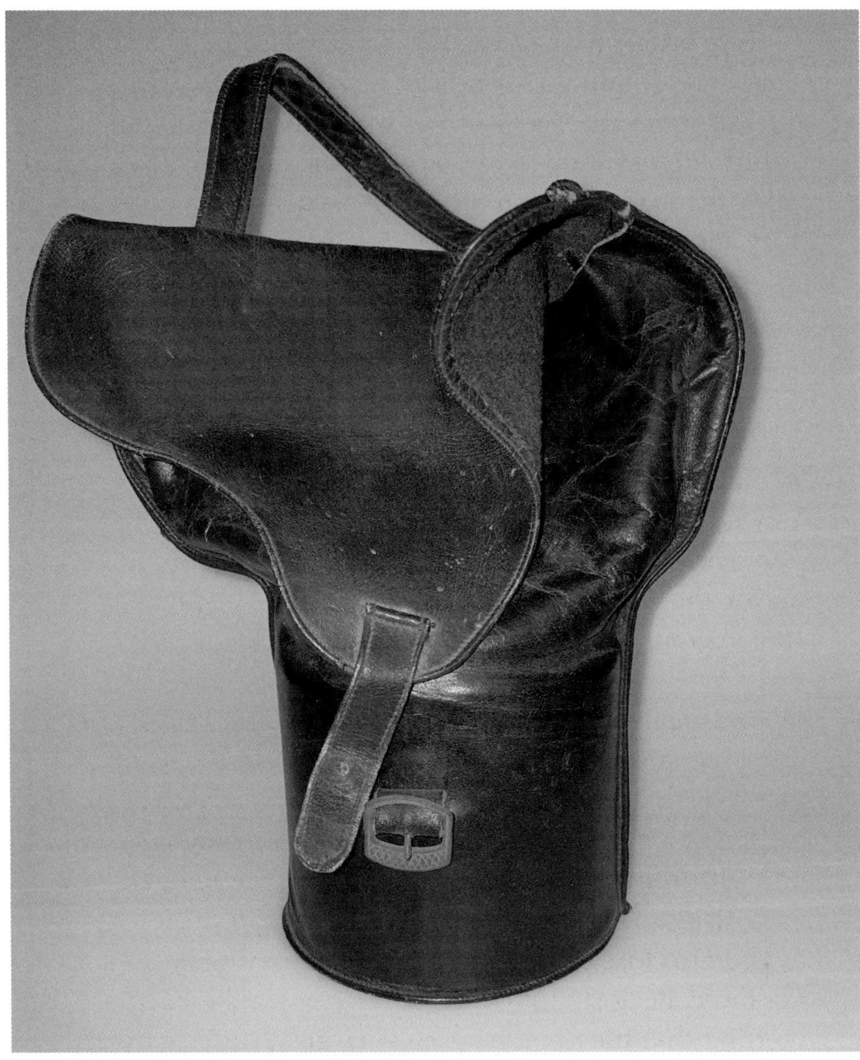

The gas mask carried by Driver Victor Green. Railway personnel were among the first civilians to receive gas masks, this one is dated 1939. (Author's Collection)

The first bomb struck LMS property soon after Dunkirk. This incident took place on 19 June 1940, when a bomb fell on the Thames Haven branch line. It landed 20 feet from the fencing, and caused damage to the banking and block telegraph. In retrospect, this was a light prelude compared with what was to follow. It was the beginning of a period in railway history which produced the most severe problems, caused the greatest amount of anxiety and demanded of all railwaymen a previously unparallelled amount of courage, tenacity, will-power and sheer hard work. From then until August, raids were spasmodic and of little account, but from then on, they rapidly increased in frequency, weight and fury, became intensive during September and reached their maximum in October. After this, they gradually tapered off until the first week of May 1941, when very heavy attacks were made on the Liverpool area. A further major assault was made on the London area on the night of Saturday, 10 May 1941, and between this date and 24 August 1940 the company had been under fire on 170 out of 260 days. On ninety-seven of those days the attacks were styled as 'heavy'.

The journalist William Forrest wrote a report about St Pancras station for the *London Daily News,* in which he spoke at length with the stationmaster. Part of the article read:

> The loudspeaker broke in on our talk: 'An air raid warning has just been sounded. Passengers can go to the shelters or proceed by their trains.' We walked out to the main departure platform. It was a daylight raid, but one of the more exciting ones, with the 'planes already over London and the guns firing briskly. There were booking offices still open – at first they used to close during raids, but now they carry on. There were the collectors punching the tickets at the barrier and forgetting that they ought to be wearing their steel helmets during a raid. Here was the guard urging passengers to get aboard the train, where they would be safe from falling shrapnel. And at the far end of the platform I could see the tin-hatted heads of the driver and firemen protruding from the cab of the engine. The driver had already arranged the special headlight code which tells the signalmen on the route that the train has already been informed of the raid.
>
> In a few minutes – while the guns were still firing into the clouds – the whistle blew, the green flag waved, and the

> 4.10 for Somewhere in England steamed slowly out of [the station]. Until the train reached the limit of the air raid zone it would keep to a maximum of 15mph. Then, on entering the All Clear zone, it would be stopped at the first signal cabin and the driver informed of the All Clear. The normal headlight would at once be restored and the train proceed without speed restrictions. If it should later run into another air raid it would be stopped again, notified of the raid, change the headlight, and reduce the speed.
>
> Inevitably the trains in and out of [the station] run late. But they keep on running. While the alarm was still on I looked in at one of the signal cabins near the station. Like all the other railway personnel, the signalmen were still at their posts. Besides their steel helmets they have been provided with steel boxes – one for each man and just big enough to hold him – in which they can take temporary cover if the bombs begin to fall perilously near … Darkness, and the night alarm. The buses stop, the taxis quit the streets. But passengers still make for [the] station by Underground, and the trains are there to take them on their way.[1]

The organisation of a vast body such as a railway might be thought of as an inverted family tree, with at the bottom many thousands of ordinary signalmen, goods clerks, linesmen, porters, firemen and drivers, above them various layers of management and finally at the top, the minister of war transport. As news of damage spread like wildfire through the chains of command, pre-arranged action would already be being taken. The man on the spot did what he could, often single handed, engineers ascertained the damage and made immediate arrangements for dealing with it, while the responsibility for the removal of unexploded bombs was under the purview of bomb disposal officers on the staff of the regional commissioners. The first problem at headquarters was to decide which job or jobs should be tackled first. The maximum number of men in

Albert William Thomas (centre), an LMS Railway Telegraph Ganger from Leicester. (Author's Collection)

the minimum period of time was the order of the day – or more often of the night.

The railway civil engineer grew used to life being a series of alarms and excursions at this time. Gangs sometimes numbering 200 men were assembled as quickly as possible and put into action, whilst stand by trains carried materials to the damaged areas. On one occasion out of fourteen lines into London, only one was available, but the main feature of railway repair work was the astonishing speed at which the trains were once more running, sometimes through the wreckage. Usually in a matter of hours craters were refilled and topped with new ashes, new lines and sleepers were laid and temporary bridges were erected. Some of the latter, particularly over water or busy street thoroughfares called for considerable engineering skill.

Normally during a raid the staff went to their shelters, but their sense of responsibility and duty was high, and often they were out before the 'all clear'. For many, they had for years taken great pride in their stretch of permanent way and day in, day out had ensured that its condition was second to none. Now this chap Hitler seemed intent on blowing it to bits, but that did nothing to alter their conviction. The signal and telegraph engineers were in a similar situation; frequently they found that telegraph and signalling wires were down, poles were smashed, colour light signals blown to pieces and many complex instruments rendered out of order. However the repair or replacement of those insignificant looking copper wires, upon which the railway relied so much for communication, was their imperative duty. Every time that there was an air raid warning, thoughts immediately turned to one or other of the company's huge junction signal boxes, operating centres, or electric power stations – which of them would be the one to sustain damage tonight? When at last the expected telephone call came in, they would soon know. In the Barking area alone, there were over 300 incidents on just 60 miles of line. One of those incidents, a small one, was recorded in the enemy action log book:

> Bomb on down bank 40 yards London side of Basildon East Signal Box. All telegraph wires down. 4 spans 24 wires. One pole broken near bottom. All glass broken signal box. Signal wires displaced and covered in debris.
>
> Supply for Repairs: Cable No. 3117, 15 pair 440 yards installed temporarily.
>
> All in work at 4.30pm.[2]

The district signal inspector for that part of the line remembered: 'We had a bellyful for months on end. But we got the communication through.'[3]

The situation which faced the train operating staff was unprecedented. A railway is like a sensitive piece of machinery, with thousands of men, engines, wagons, coaches and road vehicles all interwoven and interconnected. Damage to any part could have a knock-on effect throughout the whole system, and the very fact that any freight or passenger train ran at all at times

An LMS Railway Service badge, worn by railwaymen on everyday clothing to indicate that they were on vital war work. (Author's Collection)

seemed to the outsider to be a total mystery. The problems that suddenly presented themselves, often in a matter of seconds, when for example a big station was heavily bombed, were immense. Here, men and women fought with their pencils, their telephones, and their brains. Had they given up, then Britain's main system of transportation would have been crippled, and the life of the nation would have been at stake. For those who faced the horrors of aerial bombing the strain was unremitting and intense. A far greater degree of effort was needed for them to keep going in the face of mortal danger, than for the men of the armed forces whose training and rigid discipline had prepared them for the battle that they were to face.

In 1940, the London area suffered the most. The capital was the main target of Germany's bombers between September and October, and traffic movements were badly disorganised on numerous occasions, with many serious line blockages. Many difficulties were caused by holdups on the routes over which traffic was normally exchanged by the 'Big Four' mainline companies and the Port of London authority. This resulted in in much extra shunting to sort out the important and priority traffic for dispatch by other (often much longer) routes and the utilisation of sidings which were also urgently needed for other purposes to store the remaining traffic until it could be dealt with. Many of the heavily used residential electric services, both LMS and the London Passenger Transport Board, in North London were also often interrupted by serious blockages, whilst the damage to railway stations in general hampered traffic operations on both steam and electric systems.

St Pancras for instance, was actually hit three times in a single month. On one of these occasions it was closed for five days as a result. A large bomb shattered the greater part of the 2.5 acres of glass on the station roof on 6 October 1940. Platforms 1, 2, 3 and 4 were badly hit, and Nos. 5, 6 and 7 unusable. The two great

Damage at St Pancras after the raid of 10 May 1941. (Public Domain)

signal boxes controlling all the inbound and outbound traffic were damaged, and it was impossible to work trains from any part of the station. On one occasion a bomb which hit the Broad Street viaduct high above ground hurled an LMS wagon onto the roof of Liverpool Street station, where it had to be cut up in situ before it could be removed. Meanwhile on 19 October, at Euston station incendiaries set fire to the roof of the Great Hall, and high explosives made a crater between platforms 2 and 3, damaging the station roof, offices in Drummond Street and the west wing of the Euston Hotel. Occasionally – very occasionally – there would be a lighter moment, and one of these occurred on 14 October. For many years LMS had been the custodian of an unusual item of left luggage. Since 1876 the company and its precursors had been in possession of Ossian, a fake fairground show piece, reputed to be the fossilised remains of a prehistoric giant, as a result of a dispute between two showmen who each claimed to be his owner. An appeal to the courts to secure his disposal against mounting storage costs failed, and at 8-feet tall and weighing nearly 3 tons, for over sixty years Ossian had enjoyed a tranquil existence firstly at Broad Street and latterly at Worship Street stations. That was until that fateful night, when a German bomb shattered him into multiple pieces. Fittingly enough, the fragments were used to fill in the crater caused by the bomb that had brought about his demise; at his interment there were no mourners, one railway official observing that it was an ill wind which blew no one any good.

On the lines there were many near misses and miraculous escapes. On 15 October at 19.45, a bomb fell on the line in front of

Alfred Hobdell, an LMS Carman from Bethnal Green, received the BEM for rescuing horses from a burning stable. (Author's Collection)

the 19.30 express from London to Inverness, hauled by Royal Scot 6122 *Royal Ulster Rifleman* which ran into the debris. The engine and several coaches overturned, and the driver and firemen were injured but survived. About forty minutes later a second bomb exploded a short way ahead, blasting the retaining wall onto the electrified tracks towards Kensal Green station. At the moment a bomb struck the LMS main line bridge at Rose Lane, Berkhamsted, on 16 November 1940, the Glasgow to Euston

Above: Leonard Armitage of Hackney aboard his engine during wartime. Note the anti-glare curtain. (Ivy M. Armitage)

Left: Leonard Armitage. He was a Cleaner Passed for Firing. (Ivy M. Armitage)

express was approaching. From marks on the engine, it appeared to strike the bridge as a main girder fell. The engine and the first seven coaches were derailed and travelled 200 yards before stopping, but amazingly there were no casualties.

Among the company's personnel who were in the firing line was Leonard Armitage. He was born in London in 1920, and came from a railway family. His father was a guard with LMS and his two elder brothers also worked for the company. He also wished to join and to eventually become a driver, but at the time he left school there were no vacancies, so he took a job as a delivery boy which involved cycling all over London. He continues:

> In late 1937 I was contacted by the LMS and taken on at Willesden Sheds as a cleaner, but in 1938 I was compulsorily transferred to Camden Sheds. Late in 1938 I was put off with about sixty others and for a few months worked in the packing department of Peto Scotts packing radios. In June 1939 the LMS called me back to Camden as a cleaner, whilst there I soon became a passed cleaner after answering questions put to me by the Supervisor, this enabled me to be used as a fireman if required. September 1939 saw the start of the war, I was called up for a medical and passed A1, however, I was not allowed to enlist as I was in a reserved occupation. Even though only a passed cleaner I began to get more and more firing jobs. As it can be imagined the railways and their depots were prime targets for enemy action, but work never stopped even during raids.
>
> Camden Sheds served Euston Station, we had both passenger and goods trains in the very extensive marshalling yards, where the trains were made up which went up to the North. I did some passenger work but was mainly employed on goods trains. A few of my jobs involved staying or lodging as it was called. You worked a train up North stayed overnight and then worked another train back down.

I can recall two rather different incidents from those very hazardous days. The first occurred in the early hours of one morning as my driver and I were walking to Euston Station to relieve a driver and fireman of a train from up North. We were asked by a steel helmeted policeman to 'please cross the road and walk on the other side.' There were two bodies lying on the pavement which had apparently been hit by shrapnel. The second incident was for me the most memorable of the war. It was May 11th 1941, the worst ever raid on London. Camden Yard was being bombarded by both high explosives and incendiaries. We had many ammunition trains waiting to move out. The Regulators office, which at the time also contained eight shunters, received a direct hit. My driver and I went to see if there was anyone still alive, but there was nothing we could do. We just had to carry on as best we could without a Regulator or shunters. For this my driver received the George Medal and I received a commendation, which I still have.[4]

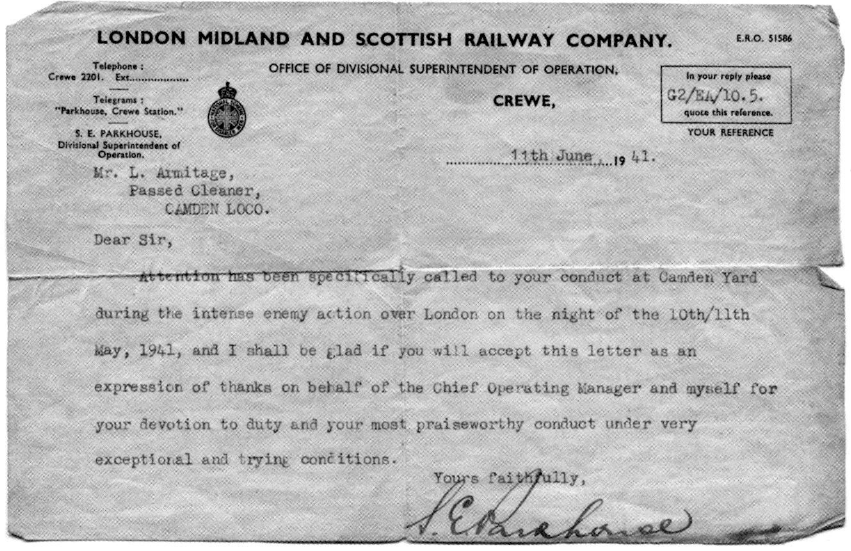

LONDON MIDLAND AND SCOTTISH RAILWAY COMPANY.

E.R.O. 51586

Telephone: Crewe 2201. Ext..................

Telegrams: "Parkhouse, Crewe Station."

S. E. PARKHOUSE, Divisional Superintendent of Operation.

OFFICE OF DIVISIONAL SUPERINTENDENT OF OPERATION,

CREWE,

In your reply please G2/EA/10.5. quote this reference.

YOUR REFERENCE

11th June 1941.

Mr. L. Armitage,
Passed Cleaner,
CAMDEN LOCO.

Dear Sir,

Attention has been specifically called to your conduct at Camden Yard during the intense enemy action over London on the night of the 10th/11th May, 1941, and I shall be glad if you will accept this letter as an expression of thanks on behalf of the Chief Operating Manager and myself for your devotion to duty and your most praiseworthy conduct under very exceptional and trying conditions.

Yours faithfully,

S. E. Parkhouse

Letter of thanks sent to Passed Cleaner Leonard Armitage by LMS management. (Ivy M. Armitage)

Alex Scott had joined LMS in 1937 at Camden Motive Depot, aged 16. In the hierarchical world of the railways, he started as a call boy; he held this lowly grade for a year before being promoted to cleaner. By the time that the war started, he had reached the position of fireman. He recalled that the coming of war greatly changed the atmosphere on the railways. All lights had to be blanked out, the side windows were painted over with black paint, and canvas curtains were hung between the cab and tender. Yet despite all these precautions, it was really impossible to prevent all glare from an engine as there were the ash pans to take into account and the side space between the cab and the tender. No fire hole door would close up tightly enough and after a time the canvas sheet would fray at the eyelets, so there was no place to put the hooks from the tender, which held the sheet in place. On one occasion he was required to work a train to Blackpool. The journey itself was uneventful, and after leaving the shed, he made enquiries as to whether he was to work another train the next day. Instead he was told to travel in the next available London-bound train. He found a seat in a guard's compartment and thought he was in for a comfortable ride until a horde of armed forces personnel entered the compartment. He ended up seated on the floor and had just begun to drift off into a doze when he became aware of a jolt and a peculiar smell, followed by groans coming from every direction on the train, but there was no shouting or screaming. He continued:

> When we looked out it was early morning, the train was at a standstill, and when I began to focus properly on the landmarks around us I took in the familiar buildings and knew that we were standing near Queen's Park, London, on the up-line. What had taken place was an air raid, and we were told that a land mine had exploded just under a quarter of a mile away. The explanation of the peculiar smell was cordite. The blast had halted the train, the fireman had been badly burnt, but the train seemed to

> be intact and we had been given instructions not to leave it. There were one or two minor cuts and nosebleeds in our sector but nothing serious. I myself felt all right and then, after a lot of outside movement and instructions, we moved off slowly and that is how we went all the way to Euston. Little did we know what had taken place on the rest of the train until we entered number 1 platform and saw about twenty-five ambulances all lined up, waiting for us to come to a stop.
>
> As we stepped off the train, the nurses from the ambulances made their way to all of us to see if any medical attention was needed. What puzzled me was what all those ambulances were doing there. As I made my way towards the rear of the train I discovered the answer. Approximately five coaches, making up the middle of the train, were completely empty of any glass. There were passengers seated inside in all different types of posture and I was just about to talk to one of them when the ambulance man told me I would be wasting my time, as he had died in the blast. It was like looking at wax figures at Madam Tussaud's, and it was very upsetting. At the time it was impossible to believe what was happening, especially to a youngster like myself. I felt a great shock and sadness for what had happened and I made my way back to Camden shed, along the tracks, in a kind of dream![5]

Scott found that one of the most frightening moments in an air raid was when, after being relieved by another crew member after a turn of duty, it was time to walk back to the depot and home whilst the anti-aircraft guns were still in action. Shrapnel would be dropping all around, and at times this was worse than the bombing. The shrapnel consisted of pieces of shell about the size of a thumb, and the nearest he came to being struck by a piece was when a small fragment caught the side of his steel helmet and made a sizeable indentation in it.

Driver Victor Green of Wigston, near Leicester. He was with the LMS throughout the war, and was often away from home for days at a time, his family having no idea where he had been sent. (Author's Collection)

The first raids in the Birmingham, Coventry and Wolverhampton area were made on two consecutive nights, 25 and 26 August 1940. They were fairly heavy, but attacks were intensified in October and November when the district control office, the district passenger manager's office, the parcels office and various signal boxes were all badly damaged. This resulted in traffic movement being seriously interrupted, and though train services were restored again in a very short space of time, other sections of operating department frequently had to wait. At Birmingham Central, for instance, the working goods shed and warehouse were completely destroyed and it was two years before even temporary replacements were provided.

Then came the devastating attack on Coventry, on 14–15 November, which shocked the entire country. LMS was also 'coventrated' (to use the German expression) during this supremely destructive raid, and at various points it received such a hammering that it brought operations almost to a standstill. Many bombs fell amid the stations, yards, and running lines, and along with the rest of the service the signal and telegraph equipment suffered considerably. This was the best example of a focussed attack on a limited target that was carried out by the Nazis in the campaign against Britain. Within a few hours 122 incidents had occurred on the railway itself, and what repercussions this entailed can be appreciated when it is remembered that the town lay within a triangle of lines, one side of which carried the main route from London to Birmingham and the Black Country. At least forty high explosive bombs were dropped on one track alone, some craters measuring up to 60 feet in diameter, and a small calibre bomb fell on to a reinforced concrete bridge, damaging the arch and parapets. Special gangs of men were dispatched from Rugby and Nuneaton, and the line was reopened for traffic a week later on 21 November. It was a remarkable feature of the repair operations that in this, the most concentrated attack that LMS experienced, the main line was restored for traffic in four days and all lines in a fortnight.

Harry Cook worked for LMS at Coventry station during the Blitz on the city. He was a parcel delivery driver. (Margaret Bowden)

No raids of note occurred during January, February and March in the West Midlands but there were four in April and May 1941. On 9 April, Birmingham was again the main target, with more main line blockages and three goods depots isolated. In this busy district as elsewhere, signal boxes were frequently hit and damaged. An example of what this meant in practice comes from a signal and telegraph engineers' department report, following a hit on the largest signal box at Birmingham New Street during this raid:

> This signal box – 76 feet long and fitted with a 152-lever frame – had practically the whole of its lower storey brickwork demolished, and the superstructure damaged beyond repair. Blast also destroyed about 40 levers, the instrument shelf, block instruments, telephones, batteries and relays. The following morning arrangements were made for complete possession of the running lines and for the clearing away of 40 wagon loads of debris. At the same time a nearby signal linesman's room was fitted up as a temporary blockpost, and provided with the necessary instruments and field telephones so that the train service could be maintained. Two emergency signal boxes – each 43 feet long – were then brought in by rail and fitted up, 40 new levers being added and the whole frame relocked. After considerable alterations, rebuilding and the installation of gas lighting the points were coupled up to the levers which remained, and the signalman was back in his box eleven days after the incident. Complete restoration was effected some days later. During the time the box was out of commission ground staff operated the points and hand-signalled trains under instructions from the temporary blockpost.[6]

Fireman Dennis Grogan of LMS lived not far from the Monument Lane depot in Birmingham. With the outbreak of war, many passenger services were cancelled, and so some drivers and firemen found that they had slipped down the promotion ladder. This was what had happened to Grogan, and he found himself back as a fireman in the control link, after previously firing in the mixed traffic link which included a fair amount of passenger work, which he preferred. The control link, at the depot, meant that he was on call every twelve hours after the end of his last duty, until a forty-eight hour working week was completed. One such call to duty came by way of the 'call boy' one evening during the nightly blitz on the West Midlands. Due to wartime regulations, the destination was not revealed by the 'boy', indeed he probably did not know himself. As Grogan bid his wife goodnight and set out into the dark winter evening, no air raid siren had yet sounded, but the bright clear moonlit sky suggested that the bombers would not be long in coming – conditions were ideal for them, and on many nights previously the bombs had come before the sirens.

As he reached the blacked-out shed, the running shift foreman, Harry Marshall was apologising to his driver, Ted Lamb, that the only engine that he could offer them for the job that night was No. 7363, a 'Jinty' (officially known as the Fowler 3F class, the Jinty locomotives were a class of small, tank engines that were designed for shunting and local freight duties). He added that traffic control had instructed that all excess north-labelled wagons standing at Monument Lane goods yard were to be taken to Bushbury sidings, and thereafter forwarded to Crewe for marshalling. All were aware that a Jinty's coal and water capacity was not sufficient to get them as far as Crewe freight sidings with a heavily laden goods train, so it was decided that Bushbury was as far as they could go, and here another crew with a Super 'D' would take over. The preparation of No. 7363 for the journey had to be done by the light of a shaded hand lamp. No naked lights could be shown outside of the cover of the shed building. On checking the sand boxes it became clear that they were empty, and Grogan discovered that there was none available that night – a frequent occurrence during the early part of the war.

These engines were notorious for slipping, when loose-coupled, and without sand this would cause the wheels to lock. But wartime shortages had to be accepted, and so Grogan and Lamb had to take the engine as she was; the absence of sand made air raids all the more terrifying for locomotive crews because when the engine threw fire into the sky, sand would have prevented it. With the sky so clear that night, the pair proceeded with extreme caution, making sure that the anti-glare sheets covered as much as possible of the footplate, before opening the firebox door to stoke up. As was common in those days the anti-glare curtains were damaged in places, offering a beacon to any passing enemy bomber in the darkness, so the usual procedure was for Lamb to watch the sky whilst Grogan fired.

A further batch of wagons was picked up at Soho sidings. Whilst there, Lamb shouted across to the yard shunter, Arthur Nash, to enquire if there was any sign yet of enemy planes. Both he and the signalman shouted back that there had been no sirens heard so far that night. Reassured by this, Grogan started to spread the coal around inside the firebox, in order to give the train a lift on the rising gradient to Spon Lane station. Suddenly Lamb barked out, 'Shut the bloody firehole door, Jerry's here!' Fires had already started around Avery's Soho Foundry (which was now producing heavy guns for the war effort) and at the nearby gasworks, illuminating the scene. The train however was now beginning to slow, and it was obvious that they would not reach Spon Lane unless the firebox was recharged. In addition to anti-glare sheets, railway-issue winter coats were also used to try to further shut out the light from the firebox. Even so, on a small engine like the Jinty, Grogan had to open and fill the box several times before reaching Spon Lane, opening and closing the door as quickly as possible each time. When they reached Spon Lane Grogan remembered:

> How many times I prayed that night I do not know, but I prayed hard at that moment that the bombers above had

> not seen us or our smoke. It was obvious that the immediate area around Spon Lane and Smethwick was receiving a 'pasting' by the looks of the many fires now burning. Reaching Spon Lane station, Ted said, 'Wind the hand brake on, the starter signal at Oldbury station is on.' Now, winding the hand brake on a 'Jinty' is a very tricky job. Only the right amount of tension has to be applied – too much and the wheels would lock. It was evident that no way would we be able to stop at Oldbury's home signal with the weight of the train. We sailed past some half the train's length, but with Ted's skilful application of the steam brake, brought the train to a halt. Walking back to the signal box to enquire why we had been stopped, and to carry out Rule 179, the signal man explained that we were to back into Spon Lane Basin goods yard, to clear the mainline for a passenger train from New Street station to pass. The passenger train was the 10.10pm, Holyhead Mail, which was still running in spite of the bombing. By this time our boiler was low on steam and I explained to the 'bobby' that we would need a few minutes to gain sufficient steam to shunt the train up the gradient into the yard at the Basin.[7]

The sound of ack-ack fire was by this point continuous, indicating that the raid was at its height. With enough steam now, Lamb began to push the train back into the Basin. However the shunter in the yard was equipped only with a small hand lamp to give signals, and in the gloom he was hard to make out. Just as Lamb was telling Grogan that he would have to get out and relay the signals to the cab, there was an almighty jolt almost like a derailment, which threw the two backwards into the steel sheets of the coal bunker, and sent the fire irons clattering down onto the tracks. Apart from shock and bruises, driver and fireman were uninjured. They screwed on the handbrake and applied the steam brake, and when the train came to a halt they jumped down onto the track to investigate what had happened. Walking one on each side of the train, it was Lamb who called out first, shouting that he had fallen in a hole. By torchlight, Grogan was able to see that he was in a bomb crater. Having helped him out, they walked on further to see that the sheds were on fire, and the light from the blaze revealed that the train was wrecked. Wagons were on their sides, with contents strewn around. Goods wagons on the adjacent tracks had also been damaged. As they reached the burning sheds they found the shunter and the guard, watching helplessly as a stable block containing half a dozen horses blazed furiously. They had tried, and failed to save the animals.

They were acutely aware that as things stood, they were fouling the main line, so the immediate priority now was to return to the cab and collect the detonator bag. A detonator was a small flat cylinder, placed onto the rail and clipped into place. When a train ran over it, the force of the wheel caused the detonator to explode, creating a very loud and distinctive sound which the driver of the train should immediately identify as being a detonator, stop his train and investigate the situation. The purpose of this was to warn of danger; detonators formed part of what was known as 'emergency protection' which on the railway refers to the method of trying to prevent any approaching trains from colliding with or becoming involved in an emergency situation which has already taken place, primarily a train accident. Grogan began walking towards Spon Lane station, in the down main line, placing detonators at quarter-mile distances.

Suddenly he came across a stationary local passenger train on the up main line, with the passengers looking out of the blacked-out windows. It was a class 4 freight engine, leaning at an angle, apparently undamaged, but with little or no ballast under the rails. It was clearly another victim of the evening's bombing. He shouted to the crew in the cab, who turned out to be a set of Bushbury men who said they were working the last local train from Stafford. Between them they agreed that the best course of action would be to get the passengers off the train and walk them down the line to the nearest air raid shelter. Some were too scared to leave the train at first, but with persuasion from the others they all disembarked – not an easy task without a platform, it being a height of nearly 6 feet from the compartments to the ballast, but the passengers assisted each other, and were soon on their way to safety. With this accomplished, Grogan finished putting the detonators at half and three-quarters of a mile from the scene. When he reached the latter point, he placed the remaining detonators at 10-yard spacings. Looking then to the up main line, in the moonlight he noticed a section of misshapen rails, with a small crater underneath. At this point, the line reached the top of a viaduct, and further examination revealed that a bomb had hit the line without exploding. Continuing in flight it had punched a hole in the wall of the viaduct and come to rest on the tow-path of a canal which passed underneath it. This would effectively close the main line from New Street station.

As the bomb was liable to be a delayed-action device and therefore likely to go off at any time, Grogan returned as quickly as possible to the engine, meeting Ted Lamb, the guard and the shunter on the way. By rights they should have taken cover in an air raid shelter, but as these were unheated and the night was bitterly cold, they decided to risk waiting with the engine, where at least they would be warm. Bombs were still going off, and one blast came from the direction of the viaduct, so Grogan volunteered to go back up the line and investigate. Sure enough, when he looked over the wall of the viaduct a large section of the tow-path had gone and the water from the canal was now lapping at the base of the wall. They reported this information to railway control via the Oldbury signalman, and were eventually told to salvage what was left of their train, obtain a new goods brake from Oldbury yard, and then proceed to Wolverhampton station where a Bushbury crew would relieve them. From there, they had to take a public service bus back to Birmingham. Both Grogan and Lamb agreed that they had had a very close shave, and as it had been one of the heaviest raids of the war so far, they

Dennis Grogan's Jinty, photographed after the war in BR livery as 47363. (D.Grogan)

wondered if their houses would still be standing when they got home.

On one occasion Alex Scott and his friend Bill Robertson, a quiet Scotsman of 6 feet and 6 inches, were to work the 20.30 evening train to Birmingham, with twelve coaches, which because of wartime restrictions on services were packed. They were to be relieved at Rugby and work back to Euston with a parcel train. He described part of the journey into the South Midlands and some of the difficulties imposed by the wartime blackout:

> Decided to take a swig of tea from the old bottle, a few minutes to sit down, just a small break. We are going a fair old rate, I should say something like 70 mph, according to the joints in the rails, and then it's through Wolverton station, a pull on the whistle and we are through before you know it. Up we get again. More shovelling and we will soon be about to pick up water at Castlethorpe troughs … this is all taking place in complete darkness as all the signs had been taken away, its left to the driver to find an object to tell him

> when to put the scoop down. A shout from Bill and down we go then, after a few minutes, up we come with a full tank. Again, a shout from Bill saying he thought he heard an air raid siren. We commenced to close the cab windows, which were then painted black, and kept the fire hole door closed as much as possible. When you did start to fire it was like two searchlights between the cab and the tender, which was one of the hazards in those days.[8]

In the Merseyside area there were six fairly heavy raids in September 1940, one in October, and another in November. The year ended with a particularly heavy attack on Liverpool, on 20 December. On this occasion damage was caused to Lime Street and Exchange passenger stations and also to Canada Dock goods station, which was flooded to a considerable depth owing to the bursting of the banks of the Leeds-Liverpool Canal. The station also caught fire but it was not possible to utilise the water in order to put it out. The most serious consequence of this raid, however, was the damage inflicted on the arches near Exchange station, which blocked the lines and isolated the facility for over three months. It was a difficult and testing time for LMS staff, because the Luftwaffe was back the next night and the one after that, with warehouses, goods offices, and loading quays being gutted, records destroyed, and 130 wagons put out of action. January and February were by comparison fairly peaceful months, but the enemy returned on 12 March as well as on the following two nights, in considerable force, causing damage at thirty-one places including fifteen blockages. Worse was to come however, for on consecutive nights, 1 May to 7 May, there was a series of concentrated attacks mainly on Liverpool and Birkenhead, though with visitations at Barrow-in-Furness and other parts of Lancashire. Here again, damage was considerable and blockages numerous.

During this series of attacks a munitions train arrived in Liverpool late in the evening of 3 May – too late to be accepted

Damage at the LMS Goods Depot, Canada Dock, Liverpool. (Public Domain)

at the docks. It was then shunted back to the nearest available sidings, which was a compromise between being safely away from the docks, but near enough to get on with the job of unloading in the morning. The Breck Road sidings, about 3 miles away, were deemed most suitable, although they were dangerously close to civilian housing. Around midnight, a bomb landed on the track next to the munitions trucks, and soon set them alight; then the trucks began to explode one by one. The courage of the railwaymen in situations like this was by now legendary. They worked until they dropped from exhaustion; they were wounded, scalded, and burned and yet they carried on. They cheated death on countless occasions to save property, passengers, and the lives of their own comrades. Others, less fortunate, were killed outright at their posts. Yet overall they never lost sight of the primary duty of the railways – to keep the country moving at a time of overwhelming national emergency, and this was a prime example of that. Numerous railway staff were to be honoured by His Majesty the King for their part in this incident, which is described below:

During the height of a raid, a munitions train stabled in a siding in the Liverpool district received a direct hit from a high explosive bomb. For several hours, ten Liverpool men, led by Goods Guard George Roberts, worked at the risk of their lives. Regardless of danger from continuous explosions in the munitions train and from high explosive bombs which continued to fall in the vicinity, Roberts and his mates strove to minimise the danger and restrict the damage.

Goods Guard Roberts, with Goods Guard Peter Kilshaw and Shunter Evans, were the first to go into action. Wagons were ablaze from the explosions and Roberts quickly realised that unless something was done, the fire would spread. He and his colleagues started to uncouple wagons immediately in front of those that were burning.

While they strove, other help was on the way. Driver Robert Bate and Fireman George Wilkinson, together with Goods Guard James Edward Rowland were on duty in a nearby siding. Immediately they volunteered to proceed to the scene and succeeded in drawing wagons in adjacent sidings away from danger. Driver Alexander Ritchie and Fireman William Frederick Fowler also volunteered to take a light engine to the scene and they assisted in drawing wagons on to roads away from the actual fire. Goods Guard John Guinan assisted in the work of uncoupling wagons so that they might be drawn away to safety.

Before the first engines on the scene could get to work, the drivers had to be given the road; and here Goods Guard Kilshaw came into action again. With considerable initiative he obtained access to the yard box, which was closed, and after studying the diagram, set the road for the engine to run into the sidings. Later, after he had returned to his depot, Kilshaw volunteered to work the fire train to the sidings and again operated the levers in the box.

For the final phase of this night's heroic story, we must go to Signalman Peter William Stringer. When the bomb

> fell on the munitions train, Stringer was standing at the top of the steps of his box, keeping a look out for incendiaries. The force of the explosion threw him down the steps and to the bottom of an embankment. Despite injury to his leg, and the severe shaking he had received, Stringer, realising the danger to traffic, endeavoured to get in touch with control.[9]

A measure of Stringer's presence of mind comes from the fact that, realising that the box telephone was disabled, he tried a public call box outside the station. When he found this also to be out of service, he set off down the road to warn the nearest National Fire Service (NFS) station, but meeting an Air Raid Precautions (ARP) cyclist messenger on the way, sent him off with the message. Next, Stringer got in touch with the ARP wardens and advised them to get people in surrounding houses into shelter. He then made his way to the next signal box to warn them to stop all traffic, before finally returning to his own signal box. Roberts was to be honoured with the George Medal for this incident, whilst Kilshaw and Rowland each received the British Empire Medal. Mrs Bessie Kelly, a grade 1 porter, was also among those officially commended for her bravery, apparently in this same incident, in November of the following year.

On all the main, branch and dock lines in the Liverpool area there were varying degrees of destruction, and some places were hit on more than one occasion. Difficulties at the docks were exacerbated by prolonged interruption to hydraulic and electric power to the cranes and capstans, and as a result of destruction at the stations, marshalling yards handling important war goods were cut off for long periods. During that difficult week, movement of freight decreased by 47 per cent, and it was not until May 1942, a year later, that the situation had returned to anything like normal.

Interestingly, the only local line not to have been included in the 1921 Grouping Act was the Mersey Railway Company, which linked Liverpool and Birkenhead, and which operated the oldest underground railway in the world outside London. Although it was independent it was none the less closely linked to the LMS network, particularly after 1938. The Mersey Railway had its own story to tell of how it beat the Luftwaffe, and continued to function in spite of enemy air action. Mr John Waddell, chairman of the Mersey Railway Company, later told shareholders at an annual meeting at Winchester House, London, some details of the bomb damage to the railway during the Blitz of 1940–1941. After discussing financial arrangements with the government, which he revealed had not been varied during the past year, and presenting the accounts again in the form approved by the Ministry of War Transport, he summarised the directors' report which had again been issued, together with a summary of the year's working. The railway was still profitable, as the net revenue available amounted to £109,976 and permitted a dividend of 2.38 per cent, on the consolidated ordinary stock. However, under the terms of the government agreement, no allowance had been made for the cost of making good abnormal wear and tear consequent on heavy war-time traffic, and this was a matter which would have to be taken into consideration when the government control came to an end.

It was then possible for Waddell to give information regarding destruction on the railway due to the war. During the late summer of 1940 minor damage was sustained, due to blast and shrapnel, but the first serious incident occurred towards the end of September 1940. A high explosive bomb fell near Liverpool Central station, and passing between two crossing timbers on the surface, penetrated the ballast. About 5 feet of concrete exploded in the tunnel between two Mersey six-coach trains stabled in the sidings. All the coaches were damaged. The next serious incident occurred one evening during the same week when a heavy high explosive bomb dropped on some houses on the south side of Beckwith Street, and penetrated about 19 feet into the ground alongside the Park Tunnel at a distance of 440 yards from Birkenhead Park station. When the bomb exploded it pushed in the side of the tunnel and blocked both the railway tracks. As a result, trains could not run between Hamilton Square and Birkenhead Park stations. The line was opened again just eight weeks after the damage. During February 1941, a bomb fell in Beckwith Street itself, making a crater on the top of the Birkenhead Park station, cutting the slope and damaging a six-coach train in the siding below. During March 1941, two landmines caused serious damage at Birkenhead Park station. The booking hall and offices were wrecked, and staircases and platform buildings badly damaged. One span of the Duke Street bridge was destroyed, and a six-coach train in the carriage-shed below was badly damaged. A large crater was made in the middle of the railway track at the Hamilton-square end of the station. The train service from Liverpool via Park to West Kirby was recommenced five days later, and the train service to New Brighton was resumed after six days. Although the station was badly damaged it was opened eleven days after the incident. In the severe raids early in May 1941, heavy damage again was sustained, but this was mostly at James Street, Liverpool. The buildings at street level were practically demolished, and whilst the station was closed to traffic for only six days, the lifts were not available until the following December. Over a period of six months, over half the company's rolling stock was damaged in one way or another, but the train service was maintained almost at full strength. The *Liverpool Evening Express* noted:

> In practically all cases when the train service between a pair of stations had to be suspended, with the co-operation of the local bus operators a shuttle service of buses was arranged to carry the railway passengers. In all this trouble, however, it is satisfactory to note that the train service between Birkenhead and Liverpool never stopped. At the same time extremely heavy traffic was handled, as at times both the Wallasey and Birkenhead ferries services were entirely suspended.[10]

Enemy attacks against Manchester meanwhile were spasmodic, with a particularly heavy raid on 22 December, when the attention of the bombers focussed mainly on the northern areas of the city. This was the first heavy raid experienced by Manchester, and there was damage to the railway network at thirty-three places. The most serious instance of damage was at Exchange passenger station where extensive fires took hold. Here, all through lines were blocked, and although by 1 January 1941 one up and one down line were functioning for trains not stopping at the station, the station itself did not reopen for passenger use until 13 January, and only then for a limited amount of traffic. Other damage in this district included several goods stations. At Ancoats, for instance, the warehouse was demolished. At London Road the stables were damaged, and a signal box burnt out, whilst at Salford telephone cables serving the divisional control office were put out of use. Manchester was again heavily bombed the next evening (23 December) with the attack reaching a crescendo at 23.45, when there was a violent explosion, apparently from a cluster of high explosive bombs. This occurred in the vicinity of platform 16 at Manchester Victoria station, where all buildings, both here and on platforms 14, 15 and 17, were either totally destroyed or extensively damaged. There was also considerable difficulty in extinguishing the resultant fires because of a failure of the mains water supply. The damage also included the total destruction of the divisional control office and many of the divisional superintendent's offices. To add insult to injury, it was then found that the emergency control office, which had been set up as a contingency in case the divisional control office should be lost was flooded, and the control telephone network had been put out of action. This double disaster necessitated the hasty rigging up of an ad-hoc control office in some nearby cellars. This in fact was one of the most serious incidents on the LMS network during the Battle for the Railways, resulting as it did in the main nerve centre of this large division being knocked out, albeit temporarily.

So much damage in such a densely populated industrial and commercial area could not help but play havoc with the extremely heavy passenger, freight and coal traffic which was then on the move, the situation being made even worse by the fact that the following day was Christmas Eve. Despite the apparent severity of the situation, by one expedient or another services were gradually restored and trains were on the move once again. This however entailed the handling of passenger traffic and much of the freight at outlying stations up to 4 miles away, and by the blocking back of a large portion of the goods and coal trains. The ripples of disruption from this incident spread far into Lancashire, Yorkshire and Derbyshire, and were particularly serious within a radius of some 30 miles.

In other cities the tale was similar. Sheffield experienced its first heavy raid on 12 December. In this incident, one man showed particular bravery. The story of his act of gallantry, along with others appeared in *The London Gazette*, and was subsequently picked up by a local newspaper in his home town of Glastonbury. He was Francis William Clark, son of Mr W. Clark, and the late Mrs Amelia Clark, who resided at King Street in the town. In his youth, Clark had played football in Glastonbury before relocating within the LMS railway company. Now, aged 47, and a parcels porter living at 32 Church Lane, Ridgeway Moor, Sheffield, he saved the life of an injured colleague during the big raid on the city in December 1940. He found his friend, a signalman, lying helpless on the goods sidings, and carried him to shelter while the raid was at its height. Despite the severity of the attack, Clark,

John William Booth, an LMS Porter, awarded the Stamp Medal from Lord Stamp for his behaviour during an air raid on Sheffield. (Author's Collection)

had set out for work at the usual time, although he had to walk over 6 miles. On the last stages of his journey the raid had been on some time, and another man was killed 30 yards from where Clark had flung himself under a wall.

As Clark crossed the sidings he heard cries for help, and searched among the debris of houses. After nearly an hour he found George Warren, the signalman, with a shattered leg, a few yards from the smouldering ruins of his signal box. Warren exclaimed: 'Thank God someone's come. I've been here for hours.'[11] Clark carried him on his back across the line towards the platform. Although Clark was only 5 feet and 3 inches in height, he got the signalman on his back and carried him towards the station. In the darkness Clark got entangled with some wires, and fell down with the casualty on top of him. He recovered, and started out again. When crossing some clear ground, a bomb fell close by and threw them both on the earth once more. When Clark at last reached the platform he put Warren under cover of some coke, and shouted for help. Warren had a leg that was broken in three places, but he made a good recovery and was later able to walk with only a slight limp. He afterwards stated that he owed his life to Francis Clark's perseverance in getting him to cover. For his part, Clark had escaped unhurt apart from extreme exhaustion. Harry Dixon, stationmaster at the Sheffield LMS passenger station, declared that the whole staff were intensely proud of the British Empire Medal awarded in recognition of Clark's gallant action. Another Sheffield man, goods porter John William Booth, received the Stamp Medal from Lord Stamp. During the raid he volunteered to take to safety horses that were frightened by falling bombs and shrapnel. He moved seven them from the danger zone, which meant walking them in the open for 440 yards. He extinguished an incendiary bomb by placing his helmet over it during one trip and also rescued his foreman who was seriously injured from an archway which had been bombed. He then helped the railway fire brigade to extinguish incendiaries, and also assisted quelling a fire. He should have gone off duty at 23.15, but worked on until 04.00.

On 15 January, high explosive bombs fell on the passenger station at Derby, killing four travellers and two railway employees. A further three passengers and five employees were injured, and the station roof was demolished for a length of 100 yards. The city was a particularly attractive target because of the extensive LMS engineering works located there. As an aside, it is worth noting that already by this point in the war they employed a high percentage of female labour. An agreement between the railway companies and the National Union of Railwaymen was made in July 1940 regarding the employment of women, and from that point onwards they began to pour in. The number of tasks undertaken by women on the railways was extraordinary. On the lines themselves women worked as booking clerks, ticket collectors, guards, carriage cleaners, stores women and signalwomen. But in the big railway engineering works they also undertook the roles of stablewoman, oiler and greaser, lorry driver, blacksmith, crane driver, oxy-gas flame cutter, electrician, fitter, hammer driver, oxy-acetylene welder, painter and policewoman. Pearl Griffiths was one of them; she remembered:

> I lived in John Street, Derby, with my mum and dad and nine brothers and sisters. On the Friday before war was declared, my dad was called up. It was very hard for my mum, as there was only my sister and I working, but we had very good aunties and uncles who were all within walking distance and also our neighbours who were very good – we all looked out for each other. In about 1940, when I was 17, I went to work in the blacksmith's shop at the railway. I had been working at Moore Eady but, due to the war, the hours were short, so I applied for a job at the railway. All the men were at war and they needed women. I went to learn how to be a hammer driver. I was the first girl to go into the smithy's

> shop. I was taken into the office to see the foreman whose name was Mr Margetts. He was a little man and always wore a black bowler hat.
>
> He took me down the shop to meet the man who was going to teach me to drive the hammer. I was told I had to have a boiler suit like the men but I wasn't very tall – 5ft 3ins – and only weighed 7st 3lbs. Somehow, they managed to get one to fit me. I also had to wear a hat as I had long, blonde hair, so it had to be covered. The man who was going to show me how to work the hammer was called Stan. The hammer was a big thing, standing in the middle of the floor. It had a long handle at the side which worked it. I was shown how to operate the handle and soon got the hang of it.[12]

March 1941 saw the Clydebank Blitz, with bombers returning to this area in April and May, but in so far as LMS was concerned, it escaped comparatively lightly, with the only severe damage being experienced in the Greenock area; the ex-Caledonian Railway 4-4-0 locomotive 14356 was destroyed at Ladyburn in this raid, the only such loss to enemy action by the company in the whole of the war. Belfast, the headquarters of LMS in Northern Ireland, suffered several small raids prior to a heavy attack on 4 May, when all the passenger platform roofs were brought down, and the inward and outward goods sheds were destroyed.

Pearl Griffiths, one of many women who undertook previously male work on the railways, at Derby LMS works in 1940. (Bygone Derbyshire)

Carriage and wagon repair and woodworking shops were also demolished, together with electrical stores, permanent way shops and other facilities. In addition, 20 passenger vehicles and 270 freight wagon suffered severe damage. The Station Hotel was also burned out except for the kitchen and a few rooms at the rear. From this point onwards however, the raids tapered off and in the remainder of 1941, there were only fifty-two further instances of damage due to enemy action across the entire LMS network.

By July 1941, although enemy action was decreasing in intensity, at least some railway workers were growing more resentful of a wartime government which seemed less than grateful for their efforts in the Blitz. The measure which especially aroused their ire was the Business Premises Fire Order which, in addition to their other duties, compelled them to become fire watchers. Its withdrawal was demanded by delegates representing 370,000 British railway workers at the annual general meeting of the National Union of Railwaymen in Swansea that month. The meeting strongly deprecated the action of the Minister of Home Security in making the order without first consulting the representatives of organised labour. It declared that firms should be responsible for the watching of their premises, and expressed opposition to compulsory measures. An amendment in these words was accepted in preference to a resolution which criticised the aforementioned minister for introducing the order before consulting organised labour, and declared that full trade union conditions should apply to employees compelled to act as fire watchers. The resolution also expressed dissatisfaction with the meagre scale of expenses laid down. Proposing it, Mr W. H. Hayter, a gateman in the East End of London, said the order had aroused more hostility than any introduced since the war. Under it, he said, one would imagine that such a thing as a worker's home did not exist. Workers were now told that their first duty was to protect industrial premises, and they were expected to leave their own homes and families to the mercy of the Blitz.

Railway workers, he added, were not prepared sacrifice the whole of their trade union conditions and rights. They were entitled to ask for the payment of trade union rates for the work they did.

Mr J. Sherer, a relief signalman of Polmadie, seconding, said they recognised that protection was necessary. There was a job to be done, and there was a rate of pay for that job. 'Then let us have it,' he concluded. Submitting the amendment, LMS employee and Labour Party member Mr William Ballantyne (Perth) said organised labour demanded to be consulted before the introduction of orders which affected its rights. He objected to men being compelled to protect the interests of people who had previously denied the workers a decent standard of living.

A 1940 National Union of Railwaymen's lapel badge. (Author's Collection)

'Fancy a railway worker earning 47s a week, plus a war bonus, being compelled to fire-watch the premises of a railway company which had fought tenaciously against any improvement in his economic position,' he added.[13]

The most remarkable aspect of this however, is perhaps the fact that there was not more significant industrial unrest, given what railwaymen had just been through. The ten months preceding this had been the most challenging and demanding in the history of the LMS company. Yet if the aim of the Luftwaffe was to paralyse the British railway system, then, as the experience of LMS showed, it was a failure. Even the massive damage to Exchange station, Liverpool and the adjoining viaduct, and to Manchester Victoria and Exchange stations were nowhere near to being operational disasters. Much of the credit for keeping the network running must go to the ready response of railway officials and staff who rose to the challenge, and in particular to the engineering, signalling and telegraph, and operating departments who co-operated fully in the task of maintaining and restoring communications.

Chapter Two

LONDON AND NORTH EASTERN RAILWAY SEES IT THROUGH

London and North Eastern Railway (LNER) was the second largest (after LMS) of the 'Big Four' railway companies created in Britain by the Railways Act 1921. It operated from 1 January 1923 until nationalisation on 1 January 1948. The total route mileage was 6,590 miles (10,610km). Of its component companies the North Eastern Railway had the largest route mileage of 1,757 miles (2,828km), whilst the Hull and Barnsley Railway was 106.5 miles (171.4km). It covered the areas north and east of London, and included the East Coast Main Line from London to Edinburgh via York and Newcastle upon Tyne, and the routes from Edinburgh to Aberdeen and Inverness. Most of the country east of the Pennines was within its purview, including East Anglia. The company employed some 180,000 personnel, and was divided into three regions, each semi-autonomous under a general manager: Southern area, North Eastern area and Scottish area. The main workshops were in Doncaster, with others at Darlington, Inverurie and Stratford, London. The company, like the others had made preparations prior to the war, in the expectation of heavy bombing. As a result with the outbreak of war, passenger services were greatly reduced; when the bombing did not immediately materialise, those service which had been cut were gradually restored, so that the timetables had to be redrawn once more.

A May 1940 photo taken at Stowmarket, looking southwards towards Ipswich and London, showing the 15.40 Liverpool Street - Norwich express headed by LNER locomotive No. 2870 *City of London*. (Copyright Walter Dendy)

Even before the Battle for the Railways began, the difficulties imposed by the wartime backout on railwaymen were immeasurable. A driver on an express locomotive had to know every inch of the road, not only every station, junction and signal but all his landmarks over 100 miles of line. When a train is travelling at 60mph there was little time to think, but the blackout meant that the countryside at night was plunged into absolute darkness, so that everything looked different. Every driver and fireman had to relearn his bearings all over again. The driver had to keep a constant watch on the road ahead, but the anti-glare curtains, aside from creating a turgid and unpleasant atmosphere, prevented him during the blackout from leaning out of his side window, so that his view was restricted to that through the front cab window. When the day's work was over, the blackout created a fresh set of problems. The first job in preparing the engine for the next day's work was to clear out the firebox, normally done outside the shed. However the burning ashes and coals made a glow that could be seen for miles. Once the blackout began, fireboxes had to be emptied inside the sheds, again creating an intolerable atmosphere. G.C. Potts was a fireman and spare driver, and remembered the beginning of the war:

> Days moved into weeks and we gradually became accustomed to the changes that had to be made in our lives. Blackout curtains had to be made and rough air raid shelters concocted before the Anderson shelters were provided. As regards the army call-up we, as locomen, were temporarily exempt. However, some of the young passed cleaners and firemen did volunteer. Before long, all engines were equipped for night time with ZEP sheets which covered the whole footplate and these at times were very hot and uncomfortable. Locomen were also equipped with a hand lamp, tin helmet and gas mask, which had to be carried at all times. Additional trains had to be run for services personnel, ammunition etc, so that you did not always get the relief that you asked for and consequently long hours had to be worked. We still worked through the links but we did not always get the specific job to which we were booked; a special might be on the doorstep when you booked on and if you knew the road you had to take it. On every engine a wash-out card rack had been fitted in the cab for the specific purpose of recording when an engine had to be washed-out, irrespective of the depot it was at when this was necessary. But the scheme had only limited success as some of the smaller depots did not have the facilities or the men to do any additional washing-out ...
>
> As Mexborough was an important place for change-over engines and traffic, we had two of the Green Arrow V2s sent from Doncaster. As no depot sends two of its best engines to another depot, one of these was a dud and with the other, you had to fight like hell to get results! I had a lot of experience with these two, working all kinds of specials; I didn't think I should ever forget their numbers but I have! About this time we were having to manage with a mixture

of coal and briquettes, which were coal dust solidified with a form of pitch. We were getting chiefly a large briquette; imprinted on the side of each was a crown and the name Cardiff, so I christened them 'Cardiff Queens'. Compared to the good Yorkshire coal we had always been used to, these were rubbish.[1]

Charles Meacher had joined LNER in 1935, as a store boy at the Haymarket shed. His father was already employed on the railway, and in order to get his son a job he simply spoke to the shed master, just before Meacher's fifteenth birthday. The family lived in the Abbeyhill district of Edinburgh, and he travelled the 3 miles to work via Waverley station. Soon he was promoted to telephone attendant and then engine cleaner at St Margaret's

An LNER train carrying Covenanter tanks passes through Newcastle, in the early part of the war. (Library of Congress)

depot, to the east of the city, before being transferred to North Berwick where he was responsible for cleaning the three engines stabled there. Later he moved again to North Leith docks. In August 1940 he was to be called up into the Royal Engineers, but for a few months experienced Luftwaffe attacks on Edinburgh, recalling that he was on his way home one night, when at the foot of Leith Walk a huge German bomber passed over Woolworths. This was followed by the unmistakable 'thud, thud' of bombs landing and exploding. The next day when he took duty at North Leith he discovered that this was where the bombs had dropped, and tenements at George Street had been demolished, causing many casualties. This was a shocking introduction to war, for amongst those killed was a girl who worked at a biscuit factory who had kept him supplied with shortbread. One bomb which exploded in the docks lifted a huge diamond crossing and deposited it in the street outside. Stone sets from within the dock area were liberally scattered, and for a while the place was a shambles. During the raid, he later leaned, the three engines at North Berwick had been moved into a tunnel for protection. Meacher remembered:

> enginemen had a measure of protection denied to other civilians. This seemed to indicate the important part played by railways in war. Part of the trainman's equipment at that time included a respirator, helmet, and badge signifying railway service, the important lines behind the lines. The helmets were black and mine was highly polished and the little brass screw at the top which kept the inside head cushion in place was sparkling too. I considered it more or less an ornament…[2]

Reg Robertson had always wanted to be an engine driver but before the war the railways were a closed shop. Only those from a railway family could expect to be employed, because the companies wanted people who were already accustomed to the long and anti-social hours that railway work entailed. The coming of the war changed all that however, as the enormous shortages of labour that they faced meant that they had to accept anyone that they could get. Robertson began as an engine cleaner with LNER but was soon on the footplate. He remembered conditions for railway staff were even worse during the war:

> The government's ruling that railway work was an exempt occupation meant that all footplatemen were exempt from call-up for military duties. All enginemen were placed under government control. They were no longer employees of a private company and they lost all the rights that went with private employment. Railway locomotive crews had worse conditions than men in the armed forces during the war. This was especially true of those in the London area who lived, worked and died under combat conditions. In the armed forces those who were directly involved with battle conditions were relieved after so many days and rested, ready to return refreshed. This was not so with the railways as they kept the strategic supplies moving day and night, regardless of weather, air raids, food supplies or any other thing that could go wrong on the home front.
>
> The only right that an engineman could demand was nine hours off between shifts. The previous shift could have extended to 20 hours without a break. The driver and fireman then went home and, nine hours after signing off, would be signing on again for the next trip which could be anything from eight to eighteen hours, depending on available relief and the position of the train at the time of relief. As if this were not enough, the crews could return home to find themselves bombed out with members of the family killed or missing. Regardless of those conditions it was report for work and make the best of it … I still

> believe that it is far easier to experience death and suffering on foreign soil instead of being blasted from one station to another in air raids that lasted up to 15 hours in the London area, and knowing that your family could be dead when you returned home at the end of the shift. Living and working in war conditions on your own doorstep is by far the greatest traumatic experience that any man can suffer and yet the footplate men in Britain during the war, and after the war, were looked upon as the dregs of society. Without them the country would have collapsed and the forces overseas would have lost their main supply column …
>
> Many of my firemen mates and drivers lived in the Stratford area and I could see them gradually being worn down by the life under fire. I have seen men lose their reasoning after coming to work and being told that a bomb had hit their home. I'll never forget one man in the coal gang. He had just started the 10 pm shift and we were standing in front of the Jubilee Shed. Heinkels were droning overhead and we heard the swish of bombs coming down. We all dived into an empty pit outside number one road and saw the skyline light up about half a mile away. The angry orange flare backed by the brilliant silver flash of the explosion lit up the entire area and we could see the jagged rooftops of houses either side of the explosion.[3]

One man in particular was aghast, convinced that a bomb had hit his house. Nothing anyone said would convince him otherwise, and he began to cry like a baby. Eventually he was taken to hospital for sedation, but he was correct, his wife and four children had died in the blast. He was unable to return to work, and was eventually committed to a mental institution.

Also among the wartime personnel of LNER was Harry Ross, who was born in 1920. Having started work as a junior porter at Chester in 1935, he was heartbroken to have failed a medical

An LNER war service badge. (Author's Collection)

at GWR headquarters at Swindon. However, a few months later there was a silver lining to this cloud when he got a job as a cleaner on the Cheshire Lines Railway, which was really an arm of the great central section of LNER. Harry was based at Chester when war was declared in 1939. He thought about joining the army, but an odd quirk meant that railwaymen who volunteered were not entitled to their jobs back at the end of the war, whereas those who were called up were guaranteed to get their old position back, so he decided to wait for call-up papers which in the end never came. Harry was a cleaner passed for firing during the Liverpool Blitz:

> I was sent with three junior Passed Cleaners to Birkenhead where we worked the engines on the docks. Most of the work was shunting freight. I remember we had Sentinel shunting engines and we had to take them across a main road now and then at a place where a policeman was permanently stationed to give you permission to cross. Those were

> incredibly busy days – everyone was fighting to get their wagons to the side of the ships. When the first bombs began to drop on the docks we would jump off the footplate and hide behind piles of sandbags. We were issued with helmets and gas masks and we wore them during a raid – strange sort of uniform for a train driver, but Liverpool was a dangerous place to be as it was very heavily bombed.
>
> We were bombed for twelve hours every night for a week. On the railways we just had to stay at work right through it because I suppose we were part of the war effort. We drove with tarpaulin sheets over the cabs so the German pilots wouldn't see the flare from the firebox. We used to work incredibly long shifts through the war. Once on a Saturday night … I was rostered to work the 8.30pm express from Liverpool to Manchester, got on the table and turned ready to go back. We were on red alert and didn't get into Warrington until midnight. We'd given a few servicemen a lift on the footplate but we had to drop them at Warrington. I noticed that suddenly everyone on the platform … had vanished. We sat waiting for the guard to give us right of way but nothing happened. After a while I wandered back to the signal box, and the signalman told me that we couldn't go on to Liverpool because the whole of the central station and the surrounding buildings had been destroyed by the raids that night.[4]

The next morning, with Liverpool still unreachable, Harry and his driver went to Brunswick yard instead. Their shift had lasted fifteen hours instead of eight, but this was not uncommon at the time. Despite the bombing, the volume of railway traffic had increased enormously with the additional demands of wartime.

The general rule was that if it was suspected that a bomb had fallen on the line, all traffic had to be stopped whilst the line was searched. Relief signalman Edward Ilsley at Potters Bar once had an express train follow him down the line while he did so, but

An LNER 04 class 2-8-0 goods engine at Gorton sheds, Manchester. The letters NE visible on the tender are indicative of wartime economies by the LNER, who painted all their loco fleet black and just used the middle initials. (Author's collection)

the express had to take its time from him. As the Blitz intensified however, the rule became harder and harder to maintain. In places like East London, with bombs falling constantly night after night, it was impossible to tell whether the line had been hit. Signalman Finch of Bow Junction remembered:

> We kept the trains moving, even though we got under the table when we heard a bomb coming. So long as we could not see an obstruction, and so long as our instruments to the next box were working, we pulled off and hoped for the best. If we had any doubt, we stopped the train and warned the driver to proceed under caution.[5]

Throughout the war, though several light LNER engines went into craters, there was only one instance of an engine pitching into the chasm left by a bomb blast whilst drawing a train, which is a testament to the care and attention with which the network was kept moving.

One of the most important targets on the north-east coast was Hull, with its vast timber wharves. This is a Luftwaffe reconnaissance photograph from 1941. (Public Domain)

In 1940, the east coast also became a target for German bombers. Some months later *The London Gazette* announced the award of the George Medal to three LNER employees for bravery during a raid on Bridlington goods yard on 11 June 1940. These men were Arthur Harrison (who had also been awarded the Military Medal in the First World War), chargeman asphalter, George William Whitehurst, labourer, both of Hull, and Ernest Victor Barker, ticket collector of Bridlington, and the incident was described as follows:

> Harrison and Whitehurst were on duty with other men when an air-raid took place, and high explosive bombs fell on a goods shed, causing casualties, damage, and fires. Harrison took the lead and, with Whitehurst, searched the goods shed which had been damaged to see if anyone had been injured. On being informed that there a wounded

> soldier in the goods yard and another in a van, they hurried to the spot and removed the wounded from the vicinity of a burning ammunition waggon containing shells which were exploding. They also entered the van in which the other injured soldier lay and which was on fire, but found that he was dead. Barker, with two other men, manned the fire-fighting appliances. The fire spread to some waggons, one of which contained live anti-aircraft ammunition. Although shells were exploding the three men continued to play water on the waggons. Three lengths of the company's hose were punctured by shrapnel while being used by the men. Two other Bridlington LNER workers figure in a list whose names have been brought to notice for brave conduct in civil defence. They are E. Pickering, motor driver, and W. Robinson, porter.[6]

Barker was later interviewed by a journalist, and added:

> I had the nozzle, and the others were at the hydrant behind me. I found the hose suddenly starting to leak in several places. Things kept flying past my head, but I did not realise at first that they were shell splinters. These were what was causing the leaks in the hosepipe. It was pretty hot, but I did not notice it much. I went on standing there and then I noticed the other two men had gone but I went on until the chief officer of the fire brigade came and told me I had better go, so I went home. There was nothing in what I did, the other men with me or the fire brigade deserve medals more than I do.[7]

In the London area the worst day experienced by LNER staff was 7 September 1940, the first of the big German raids. During the afternoon, Channelsea carriage sidings were hit, and carriages set on fire. However, shunters quickly got to work clearing the debris and, in the end, only fourteen carriages were lost.

Above left: G.W. Whitehurst, an LNER employee from Hull, awarded the George Medal for helping to rescue a wounded soldier.

Above right: Arthur Harrison, an LNER Maintenance Sub-Ganger from Hull, awarded the George Medal for assisting Whitehurst.

During the same afternoon, all the Cambridge lines were blocked at London Fields. Two signal boxes were destroyed and lines blocked elsewhere. The bombing continued into the evening and through to 01.00. After the bombing had eased the assistant district superintendent at Stratford went to inspect the situation. He found that the lines were intact through Stratford itself but the signals had failed. The drivers and firemen had stayed with their engines throughout the bombing, but all were now stranded. One by one the superintendent and an inspector guided the engines out by means of torchlight.

Another bad night for Stratford came on 24 September, when Bow Junction was hit and all lines into Liverpool Street were blocked. The service into London was maintained by reversing trains at Stratford and diverting them via other routes. More ingenuity was shown when a bomb fell one night at Chobham Farm, just at the point where the engines come out of the sheds and on to the main line. All the outlet roads were completely destroyed except one, and even in this case the rails and sleepers had been distorted by the blast. Thus, the engines needed for the day's traffic were effectively bottled up. Fortunately, among these was one of the heaviest express engines in the company, and by coaxing this out gently the yardmaster was able to flatten the buckled rails and sleepers back down. The remaining engines followed it out in procession. The following night two landmines came down, one near Finsbury Park and the other at Harringay. The latter went off a few hours later but the former was not dealt with until the following day. They caused enormous disruption to passengers trying to reach King's Cross, but London Transport stepped in by offering the affected passengers free travel on the tube and a fleet of buses. Barnes station was hit on 12 October with one passenger killed and seven staff injured, including the crew of an LNER freight train to Feltham which had been shunted on to the up local platform, probably to turn around as a result of the damage at Syon Lane. During the worst of the 1940 attacks on London, much of the pressure was taken off the city's rail network by the Cambridge district. Its operating superintendent, Gerry Fiennes, wrote afterwards:

> The London Blitz we could see nearly every night. Spangles of yellow and white and red tracing the southern sky. [We] naturally [tried] to do as much of London's work as we could. We wanted to get wagons into and out of London just as quickly as we could. The Cambridge District therefore trapped everything for London, shunted it over and made direct loads to the final terminal. Not only that but we held the traffic until London was ready to unload. We were also the diversionary route for traffic avoiding London. Colchester-Ipswich-Bury-Cambridge-Bletchley-Honeybourne-South Wales was used to capacity. Luckily when the Colonel built Whitemoore mechanised Up and Down Yards he did not pull up the yards that they relieved. We still had an Up and a Down Yard at Whittlesea. Ely was half empty. The three yards at Cambridge were little more and we added a fourth by expanding the Royal Show Ground Sidings at Trumpington. The Cambridge District shunted the lot. Ben Mitchell, Jimmy

A German Heinkel He111 photographed shortly after crossing the British coast on a daylight raid, 1940. (New York Public Library Collection)

> Hulme, Albert Chapman, Jimmy Lord, Percy Baines and the rest under the benevolent and ingenious direction of George Docking saved London from grinding to a halt. Nothing was ever too difficult. We never said 'can't'.[8]

Interestingly, Fiennes believed that the German bombers never deliberately attacked marshalling yards, the Luftwaffe having realised that with their multiple parallel alternative lines it was almost impossible to shut them down unless they managed to hit the single inlet or outlet track – a very difficult thing to achieve. *The Scotsman* reported:

> The railway engineering staffs who have broken records over the rapid repair of air raid damage have worthy

colleagues in the operating staffs, whose job it has been … to maintain essential freight and passenger services and to devise where necessary temporary alternative routes. Numerous stories could be told of the great resourcefulness and often splendid courage with which stationmasters, inspectors, yardmasters, drivers, firemen, signalmen, porters, and the less well-known control office staffs have tackled traffic problems caused by aerial-attack. Here are a few of them concerning the LNER. On two days in recent weeks bomb damage close to an LNER main line in the Metropolitan area necessitated the use of a North London suburban station as a terminal for all passenger trains, while fish, meat and other freight traffic was dealt with at adjoining stations. Booking office staffs with stocks of tickets were rushed out to the temporary-terminal station, passengers were conveyed to and fro by emergency bus service, and their luggage by lorries put at the disposal of the LNER by the military. The world-famous '*Flying Scotsman*' express, though delayed ran as usual except that, for the first time in its long history of 78 years, it did not leave from a platform numbered 10. On another occasion bomb damage at night cut LNER lines in the Eastern suburbs, with the result that trains destined for the Metropolis over the route affected could not proceed beyond an inner suburban station. Nor could emergency bus services be arranged, for the alternative road route had also been bombed. However, by restoring damaged tracks that connected with a branch line to a suburban station on another route into London and reversing trains at that station the service could be resumed. In less than 10 hours the necessary repairs had been effected by the engineers; while to reduce the time of reversal to a minimum, the operating staffs had mobilised sufficient locomotives and crews for the working of the trains back to London as fast as they arrived at the suburban station.

> Signalmen have stuck to their posts under most trying conditions, and on many occasions have examined the lines between signal boxes, sometimes dealing with incendiary bombs on their way. Like the stationmasters, yardmasters and inspectors, who have often been called out at night to examine the tracks, and extinguish incendiary bombs, the initiative they have displayed and the information they have promptly given to the control office staffs have enabled altered working arrangements to be made within a very short time of the damage taking place. The staff who handle the working of important newspaper, mail, and parcels traffic also deserve praise, In the event of a line being closed, arrangements are immediately made with the postal authorities and newspaper officer for the traffic to be taken to other stations on alternative routes. In spite of the difficulties and delays which such changes could so easily cause the fine work of the railway staffs, often carried on during air raids, has, together with the speed with which newspaper editions have been brought to the stations, achieved an almost pre-war degree of punctuality in dispatch.[9]

One of the most isolated parts of the LNER network was Halesworth railway station in Suffolk, which was bombed on 18 January 1941 resulting in three deaths, Walter Holland, the stationmaster, Hannah his wife and their daily help, Joan Clarke. At least two-thirds of the building was demolished in this attack. Why the station was bombed is still a matter of debate today. Shortly after it had dropped high explosive bombs on an East Anglian town earlier that Saturday afternoon, a German aeroplane was seen 'hedgehopping' as it made its way towards the coast. It was apparently endeavouring to avoid anti-aircraft fire which was stated at the time to be very lively. An assistant at a country motor garage said the machine only just missed the roof. He could see the occupants of the front part, and the ice on the wings quite plainly.

Halesworth Railway station showing rolling stock destroyed in the raid of 18 January 1941. (Halesworth Museum)

Halesworth was accustomed to the dreaded wail of the air raid warning siren which was housed at the former police station in London Road. There had been countless incursions by Nazi bombers during daylight, and large formations on their way in or out to bomb British cities and towns at night. But it was not until 1941 that the stark reality of bombing was brought home to the town. One eye witness reported:

> On Saturday January 18 1941 I and the late Ted Sutherland took up our four hour duty stint at one o'clock in the afternoon at the Royal Observer Corps Post which was based on a field off Holton Road. The farm was owned by the late Reggie Page. The post comprised a sand-bagged compound with a galvanised roof. Our equipment consisted of a circular map of the district fitted on a tripod stand with a moveable pointer with which an aircraft could be sighted, followed and

plotted across the specially marked plotting map. Our post also linked up other observation posts in our area.

One of the two men on duty plotted aircraft on the map, while the other had the mobile phone, which was directly connected to our centre headquarters at Norwich, which was directly connected to Fighter Command. We could also hear other posts in our area sending in their reports to the centre. When we took up duty on Saturday January 18, at one o'clock in the afternoon, I was on a spell with the telephone. It was snowing. I heard the Southwold post report an unidentified aircraft approaching the coast. In a short time the snow ceased and we heard an aircraft approaching. This was continually reported to the centre.

Through this now very thin snow we saw the aircraft flying at about one to two thousand feet. It was a Dornier bomber known to us as the 'flying pencil'. By now the snow had stopped and the sun came through. We kept up a continuous report to the centre. The Dornier flew in and circled the town three times. It then began what was to be a bomb run. I saw it line up our post and then came a stick of bombs. There was a direct hit on the Station Master's House which was part of the Railway Station, which killed him, his wife and a young girl who worked for them.

The raider came straight for our post, possibly having spotted the searchlight which was in the same field as our post. We had to take cover in our shelter as the Dornier opened up with his machine gun. We could hear the bullets around us. We came out as he passed overhead and banked back towards the sea. We did hear that an army machine gun post at Henham opened up and hit the Dornier before it reached the coast and was seen to be in trouble with smoke coming from the aircraft as it flew over the sea. But this was never confirmed.

That night Lord Haw-Haw broadcasted from Germany that a successful raid had been made on marshalling yards

Another view of the damage at Halesworth. (Halesworth Museum)

> at Halesworth. Except for the debris, the rail line was not touched.[10]

At Tyne Dock, on the outskirts of South Shields, there was more destruction and also more bravery. Here, as would also happen at Hull, a large store of timber pit props was set on fire at the beginning of a raid on the night of 10 April 1941. Not far off there stood 300 wagons, all loaded with ammunition which was awaiting shipment. Ten of these wagons were set on fire. The ammunition began to explode, and bullets were flying out of the wagons in all directions. Six LNER men were decorated for their part in this incident: yard inspector Robert Hume (65 years of age), and driver John Steel (both of Oldham, Lancashire), who both received the George Medal; shunter Jonathan William Angus, yard inspector Charles Colthorpe, acting yard inspector Robert Stephen Ward, and assistant traffic agent G. Brown who all were awarded the British Empire Medal. Driver Steel hooked his engine on to the burning wagons and drew them for some distance down the yard, until he reached a water column. Each wagon in turn was pulled up to the column, and its fire was put out. Of the other wagons, only one – containing steel helmets – was destroyed. Steel manned his engine alone, having sent his young fireman away out of danger. These men were at work from 01.00 until 06.00, with bombs falling round them all the time. They saved most of the shipment, and the vessel lying at the dock was able to continue loading the next morning as usual. Not decorated in this incident was signalman Clark, who stuck to his post at Tyne Dock bottom box all that night through the continuing raid. He was practically in the middle of it all. 'Tremendous destruction must have occurred had the wagons of ammunition exploded,' said the official account of the action.[11]

The Luftwaffe attacked Hull in early May 1941. The bravery of one man in particular, Fred Potter, an LNER wagon examiner, of Watton Grove, North Hull Estate, was recognised through the award of the George Medal. He told reporters afterwards:

> I was on duty wagon examining, when thousands of incendiary bombs were dropped in the area. It was impossible to cope with them all, and several wagons were burnt out. A high explosive bomb burst about 100 yards away from me, but a shed sheltered me from the blast. Noticing an incendiary was ablaze on top of a timber stack, I kicked it off. I then tried to tear a tarpaulin sheet off the stack, but the tar was molten and burned my hands. It was impossible to get the sheet clear, so I went for assistance. A fireman came down, but by this time the whole stack was ablaze. Another fire had broken out nearby, but by carrying water from a pond it was possible to get this outbreak under control. To help us in this work I carried four lengths of rubber hose, a length at a time, from an auxiliary pump in a nearby street, and largely as a result of our efforts, most of a stack of between 25 and 30 tons of timber was saved. Later there

> was another shower of bombs, some of which dropped on stables. I could hear trapped horses breathing heavily under the debris, and set to work clearing their covering of beams and slates. I had to saw through some beams, and must have thrown several tons of debris away before I could reach them. I am not accustomed to handling horses, but the animals seemed to realise that I was assisting them, and they kept perfectly still until I uncovered them. I must admit, however, that there were times when I was a bit frightened, as to what they would do when they freed their hoofs. Five horses in all were taken out alive, but two of them had to be destroyed later, they had been protected from blast by some peat moss, but some smoke from a fire which had started under the debris seemed to trouble the horses.

Potter afterwards tackled a fire which had broken out on some dock staging, and his timely efforts prevented any extensive damage. He had been with LNER for twenty-eight years, and during the previous war he served with the No. 1 Light Railway Operating Company in France. He was a married man with four children, his two sons being in the army, while a daughter was attached to the Auxiliary Fire Service (AFS). The other daughter was married and living at Loughborough. The official record of the deeds for which Potter was awarded the George Medal states: 'He then saw that some wooden decking around a coal hoist was on fire. Improvising a rope by fastening together a number of

MR FRED POTTER

MEDAL FOR HULL AIR RAID HERO

Put Out Fires: Rescued Horses

Goods Checker Fred Potter, awarded the George Medal. (Author's Collection)

strong sheets, he drew water from the dock in buckets and extinguished the fire.'[12]

The centre of gravity of Hull lay in the goods warehouses and docks. The enemy were well aware of that fact and they did not miss. Among the stacks of timber at the docks there occurred some of the most terrible fires of the war. Once an engine, with its fire drawn, was marooned on a siding by a nearby bomb, with fires blazing all round it. Before the fires abated the engine's safety valve was seen to lift. The water in the boiler had been brought to boiling-point by the flames outside. In the same way, surface shelters, although they stood up well to blast, became uninhabitable during timber fires, because they simply heated up like an oven. Wilfred Filby (foreman fitter and blacksmith), Alfred Tawlks (outside maintenance foreman), and John McBain (general labourer) were on duty on the night of 7 May 1941 at the LNER Victoria Dock workshops, which was the main repair depot for the docks at Hull. Within five minutes of the alert sounding the whole yard was alight. The water-main for the pumps was broken, so they went to the fore-shore pump. But by this time incendiaries were all over the place among the timber, and they could do practically nothing. At one time they found themselves completely ringed round by fires, and had to escape by crawling out under a ship undergoing repair on the slipway. Most of the dock repair shops went except a large building known as the bungalow, which, however, was destroyed the next night. When the fires died down, the work of salvage began. Debris was cleared out of the shops, all the machines were stripped down to the bone, and then they were put on bogies and run round to temporary premises. New electric motors and shafting were put in. Within six weeks half the shop was at work again. The most serious loss in some ways was the destruction of 4,000 patterns at a time when no suitable wood was obtainable for replacements.

Meanwhile the bombers had also returned to London. LNER driver H.A. Butcher drove the 20.15 train from

Enfield to Liverpool Street on the night of 19 March 1941. He reported:

> It's funny how we enginemen get used to running through the raids. At first we were a bit dubious when we could see the gunfire and hear the planes overhead, and we used to feel a bit like stopping at the next station until they had gone over, but now we seem to take it a bit more as a matter of course, and have the one object of getting our trains safe to the end of the trip, and as near to time as possible…

After describing the first part of his journey, Butcher continued:

> We arrived at Cambridge Heath and were just leaving the platform when there was a hissing sound, which we realised was incendiaries dropping, starting fires all around us. After this it was really exciting, with the heavy stuff coming down on both sides. My mate was calling to me 'Look up!' 'Duck Down!' 'Dodge!' and goodness knows what, but this wanted doing, seeing that I had to look where I was going and also to watch the train to see that it had not been set on fire. All the same I more than once found myself taking his advice without meaning to. And more than once our tin hats clashed when we happened to duck at the same moment. We got to Bethnal Green safe and sound, and then there were some more heavy explosions. Once again I was told to duck, but I had to laugh because I thought of the caper I must have cut. My mate wanted to know what the joke was, because he could not see anything to laugh at. We stood at the platform for six or seven minutes with the signal against us and things were none too comfortable. Then the signalman came and instructed me to proceed with caution to the next signal box.
>
> I asked how much more cautious I was to be, and he told me that it had been reported that something had dropped in the section, so I said 'Well, I suppose we have got to be

> the muggins like and find it.' Needless to say we did not go down the bank very fast, we were straining our eyes to see if we could see any sign of anything, but all was well and we arrived at Liverpool Street all safe. Before we had stopped our passengers were out of the train, and it was like magic the way they all disappeared, so that when we looked round the whole platform was deserted with the exception of my mate and myself.[13]

Another driver concluded an equally hair-raising report with the words, 'I should like to say that working trains under such conditions is very trying to the nerves.' In April 1941, Holloway carriage sidings came under attack. The raid started at 22.00 hours, just as the work of shunting carriages was beginning. The whole of Holloway yard was ringed round with flares of all colours dropped by the enemy. In contrast to normal blackout conditions, there was now plenty of light to work by. The yard however received more than just flares. Incendiary bombs, many in Molotov bread baskets came down to the left and right, and numerous nearby buildings were set alight. In the yard 157 incendiaries were collected, all being successfully dealt with, and not a single coach caught fire. Driving an engine at that time required special nerve; one man, driver T.W. Rhodes taking the 19.45 service from Liverpool Street to Chingford wrote in a report of an incident which occurred on 19 April 1941:

> We were just leaving Hoe Street, when a bomb hit the West Avenue overline bridge about twenty or thirty feet away from the track. We got the blast on the engine and there were bricks and woodwork flying about, and almost at the same time another one fell on a house on the same side of the line, but just a little bit further away. I shut off and I could feel that the train was still rolling behind me and we both looked back and could see that we were not off the road because there was plenty of light from the German flares,

so I opened the regulator again, meaning to get to the next station. I thought that if any passengers had been hurt, the best place for them was at a station and not somewhere in between, but the communication cord was pulled.

I told my fireman (L. Bishop) that they must have stopped us for some purpose and he had better go back with the guard to see if anyone was badly hurt, and while he had gone I went to the telephone on the automatic signal and advised the signalman to stop the up train in case there was any obstruction on the other road. My fireman went along the train with the guard to see who had pulled the cord and to see if anyone was much hurt, and found about fourteen people cut by glass, but only one of them looked at all serious. He and the guard pulled off the doors that had been damaged and laid them on the track and pulled a few pieces of fencing out of the carriages, and then he telephoned to the signalman to have a doctor or someone at Wood Street to dress the cuts.

When he had done this he came back to me and I got right-away from the guard. The signal had been off all the time and so we drew into Wood Street. When we got there railway staff were waiting to attend to the passengers. Some were our loco men and others were station staff, and my mate went back to give them a hand.

I forgot to say that my mate was nearly a casualty himself because when the bomb went off a handlamp that was on the tray of the engine went up in the air and came down on his head. It was rather warm overhead all this time, but the flares helped a bit in dealing with the injured passengers … eventually we got to Chingford only twenty-nine minutes late.[14]

On the same evening driver J.T. Tant was working empty carriages from Liverpool Street to Stratford. At Bow Junction the signalman instructed him to proceed under caution:

> Half a train length before we reached the next box we ran into something. I was going carefully and made a quick stop. We go out and had a look to see and found that there were some steel plates all over the place, which I believe came out of the Derby Yard, although at the time we thought they had come out of Cooks soap works because there were soap wrappers all over the place, but no soap. There was nobody there to help us at that time, so we started to clear up a bit and while we were doing this Driver Caunt of Epping, who had stopped close by with an up train, told me that there was a piece of plate under the first coach of the train. We could not shift this, and I told Caunt that when he went to the signal-box he had better tell them about our predicament, and presently three or four goods guards came along from Stratford.
>
> The piece of plate under the train had got its corner stuck right into a sleeper and was bent over under the wheels, so the goods guards stopped a down carriage train and got the axe out of the brake van. I had previously had a look in our train and found that it did not carry an axe. Some Home Guards came along, and one of them was the smallest man present and so we gave him the axe and sent him under the carriages and eventually he chopped the sleeper in half and the rest of us lifted the plate away. When this was finished there was nothing to stop us any longer as we had been clearing the rest of the plates while the Home Guard was chopping up the sleeper. We reached Stratford Carriage Sidings at about 1am.[15]

There must have been many drivers who had similar experiences, but for whom no such documentation survives. Overwhelmingly their behaviour under such trying conditions reflects great credit upon them.

About a mile to the north-west of Stratford lay Temple Mills marshalling yards. Here freight trains from all over the system

A German incendiary bomb, dropped in the great raid on London of 10 May 1941. (Author's collection)

arrived, and it was also one of the main exchange points between the LNER network and LMS and Southern Railways. It was an important and obvious target for the Luftwaffe, but the 150 or so traffic men of different grades who worked there kept it going through sheer bravery and determination. Many of them were veterans of the 1914–1918 war and had fought in the battles of the Western Front, so courage under fire was not a new concept to them. It is said that fortune favours the brave, and only one man lost his life there through that terrible winter. Often during a raid there would be several trainloads of British bombs present, the total exceeding 1,000 tons. On another occasion, a train containing cannisters of poison gas stood in the yard when it was attacked. Fires were frequent, and after a string of wagons were set alight by incendiaries, the yardmaster called the local fire brigade out onto Ruckholt Bridge which crossed the yard. As each wagon was shunted under it the firemen doused it with their hose. Petrol trains also used the yard, and by good fortune none of these were ever struck by incendiaries. Once two tank wagons were pierced by bomb splinters, but they struck low down and the petrol poured out harmlessly forming a lake in the yard. A few anxious hours passed, until the fuel had safely evaporated. The worst night of all was the last of the heavy raids, 10 May 1941. By the following morning 71 out of the 158 sidings in the yard had been put out of action.

A London railway terminus was too large and important a target for the enemy to miss, and LNER's Liverpool Street hub was no exception. Like the other stations in the capital, it was bombed several times. A bomb which fell on platform 1 severely damaged a train that was standing at it, and it took several days before the wreckage could be cleared. Another bomb hit platform 4 at its outermost end, still another hit platform 18 on the eastern side of the station. A bomb which fell in Bishopsgate slightly damaged the east side booking office. The strain on the station staff was not so much from the danger as from the disruption. An inspector on duty had always to be ready to alter traffic arrangements, and to see that a train went out alright, even though there might be disorganisation. There was also the difficulty of getting home after a shift, and sometimes men used to sleep in the old, disused cloakroom on hard boards. Platelayers were on duty continuously, ready to deal with any damage which might occur on the lines near the station. Shunters went about their work, dealing with incendiaries as they found them. Signalmen continued with their work in defiance of the bombs, though it had not always been so. Some of the older signalmen had been under fire in the 1914–1918 war, but many of the younger men had not, and during an early raid they flung themselves down on the floor of the west signal box. At this moment in strode the upright figure of Colonel H.H. Mauldin, divisional general manager, Southern area. Sheepishly, the younger men got back on their feet.

Liverpool Street's worst bomb was the delayed-action device which fell in one of the engine sidings at the end of platform 10. From the traffic point of view it could hardly have landed in a worse spot. Both the east and west signal boxes were within deadly range of it, as were the turntable and engine sidings. Four trucks loaded with ballast were pushed into the siding to try to provide a screen, whist the station carried on. Unfortunately, the next day the bomb went off, resulting in two deaths. That the toll was not higher was largely due to the ballast wagons which did their job in absorbing much of the blast and being rolled back by it.

On 11 May 1941, the big block over the west side of the station was burned out, and Liverpool Street was also to be flooded out by a burst water main caused by a bomb. Water cascaded down the west side of the station, and in the booking office water was standing to a depth of 8 inches before it could be drained away. King's Cross suffered greatly from incendiaries, and on one particular night thirty-seven struck the station. On another occasion a bomb in York Road blew the radiator of a car into the station yard. During the great raid of 11 May two 1,000lb bombs which were chained together fell on the offices adjoining platform 10. Twelve men in the railway transport office were killed, but the clerks on duty in the booking office miraculously escaped. The front of the office, facing the booking hall, was demolished, but the two men were able to climb out through the wreckage of the bookstall behind them. These bombs also brought down a section of the main roof. When it fell, a girder struck the cab of a newspaper train which was standing at platform 10. Fortunately, the crew had taken shelter and were not inside. Despite this serious damage the station was not put out of action. Even the damaged newspaper train was able to run, and all scheduled trains the next day got away. The damage to the roof took a week to make stable. During the raid, shunters could take shelter now and then under the signal box, but high above them the men and boys operating the 230 levers never missed a turn of duty. Sometimes overlooked, the beating heart of King's Cross was a modest brick building – the station canteen. Here the manager and his staff kept the station personnel fed, come what may. Hundreds of men and women came in for their meals, whilst hot food was sent up to the signal box and packed lunches were prepared for the outgoing train crews.

Marylebone passenger station escaped lightly with no serious damage save for a few incendiaries on 11 May, but Marylebone goods station was not so lucky and was completely destroyed. Damage to water mains meant that apart from one wing it was completely burned out with even the food and liquor in the faults being lost to the flames. Marylebone was vulnerable however as the tunnels leading to it through Hampstead and St John's Wood were rather shallow. On one occasion a bomb actually fell right through Lord's Cricket Ground into the tunnel below, without exploding. Onlookers were astonished to see it brought out the next day, dangling from the gib of an LNER crane. On another occasion they were not so lucky, and a bomb at Carlton Hill blew a large hole in the tunnel roof into which fell the remains of three houses. The tunnel was cleared of debris by piling it into railway wagons and taking it away. No sooner had this happened however than a bomb fell in the grounds of the St John and St Elizabeth Hospital and again penetrated the tunnel, blocking it once again. Marylebone was now completely unreachable, and plans had to be made for dealing with its traffic. As part of these arrangements a temporary platform was created from sleepers at Neasden.

Further out, at Barnet, relief signalman Charles Redgers was to be awarded the British Empire Medal for his resolute conduct on many occasions. Once a bomb hit the station and with the stationmaster and others buried under debris, Redgers organised platelayers to dig them out. While they were doing so, despite communications being down he got through to Hornsey on a Post Office telephone and arranged for a crane to be sent. All this time, though lines were down, he kept the trains moving under caution. Redgers was adept at contacting other stations to get messages through to control and thus keep traffic moving.

Among the youngest of the LNER staff during the Blitz was signalman George Case, who joined the company as a messenger aged 14, after the war had begun:

> I went down to the Holloway yard master's office. In those days you had to replace someone to get a job; in other words, if someone wanted to leave the railway, or if they were joining the Army, you could take their place. If they couldn't find someone they couldn't leave. A mate of mine wanted to go into the Air Force so I jumped at the chance to replace him as a telegraph lad, which is exactly how my dad had started. I got a reference from the vicar at Potters Bar and a school reference …[16]

Case's father only realised that his son had left school after he had been at work for a month, when the school board inspector called at the house.

> [My dad] was furious when he found out. He made me go back to school till I was legally allowed to leave and start work, which was on my fourteenth birthday, 14 November 1940. This meant going back for only a short time, however, and as soon as I could I went back to be a lad messenger. I started each day at 8.30am at Finsbury Park.[17]

This job involved going down to all the platelayer's cabins and signal cabins to pick up the mail for the yardmaster. It was a hard task for a small boy, not only carrying a huge bag of messages but also having to cross backwards and forwards across the main lines, seven sets in total, with only his own sharp eyesight to protect him from approaching trains. As a concession on foggy days, someone from the shunters' yard would assist him to cross. Whilst the lad messenger was without doubt the most lowly position in the yard, it did at least give him an insight into how the various parts of the railway worked. In addition to collecting and delivering messages for the yardmaster he also worked in the stores, taking chunks of soap to the various cabins for example. At 10.30, he made tea for the entire office staff, and also ran errands. As a new boy, he was often the butt of practical jokes, for example being sent for green oil for a signal lamp. Promotion was quicker in wartime however, and he was only a messenger for six months. After this he became a telegraph lad in a signal box. The responsibilities of a 14-year-old in this role were daunting. As well as scrubbing the floor and cleaning every available piece of metal so that the interior of the signal box looked immaculate, he was also responsible for filling in the registration book detailing all movements of trains and their timings. He used the telephone and telegraph to send messages up and down the line, and it was unofficial but accepted practice that the telegraph lad would operate the levers whilst the signalman had his breakfast; this enabled him to gain familiarity with the equipment whilst the signalman was on hand if he got into any difficulty. Soon the air raids on London began in earnest:

> Sometimes I wondered why they bothered to warn us. There was nothing we could do. We just sat there like sitting targets and dimmed our lights a bit. It was mainly gas lights in those days so they were pretty dim anyway, and all the windows were blacked out with a hole left just big enough for the signalman to look out and peer up and down the line. In the back of the cabin at Holloway they fitted a steel shelter, actually inside the cabin. Old Dusty used to get nervy when there were bombers about, so he'd go into the shelter at the back of the box and tell me to get on with it. If bombs fell nearby I was supposed to dash into the steel box with him and sit on his lap – it was so small there was only room for two of us that way. It always seemed funny to me, sitting there with this great big registration book open on my knees while Dusty held up an oil lamp so I could continue to fill the book in. That metal box shelter was a complete waste of time, too. It was just a heavy steel box, so if the cabin had been hit it would have gone crashing down through the floor and we'd have been killed anyway. I suppose the idea was that it would at least protect us from flying glass.[18]

There were many near misses and one night a bomb struck the ground right in front of his box, but failed to explode. If it had gone off it would have been certain to have caused casualties. Another LNER lad, Geoffrey Raynor was a messenger boy at East Leake when war broke out. A few months later he was promoted to train register boy at Nottingham's Victoria North signal box, where his experiences were similar. He remembered:

> TR Boys were not supposed to work the signals or points or answer the Block Instruments, the means by which trains

> were accepted and passed on to other signal boxes. This was done by Bell Signalling and an instrument showing three positions: 'Line Clear', 'Train on Line', and 'Line Blocked' (this last was the normal position.) The line was considered blocked to other trains until acceptance of the train in question was given by repeating the recognised Bell signal, ie four beats on the Bell indicated an express passenger train was being offered. However, as I became more conversant with the Block instruments and lever frame (where the levers were connected to points, lock bars and signals), the Signalman would let me answer the Block Bells and move the levers whilst he had a cup of tea and a bite to eat.
>
> Located within the Victoria North signal box were two steel cabinets or shelters, one for the Signalman, and one for the TR Boy to take refuge in during air raids; each cabinet had a door and the top was also hinged. That worried me; I thought any blast would push me through the top. The cabinets were to protect the signal box staff from flying glass; signal boxes at this time were built with glass windows on all four sides.
>
> I remember when an air raid was in progress on one occasion, sometime between 7.30 and 9 o'clock one night; the anti-aircraft guns were at their height and bombs were falling. Bill, the Signalman was in his shelter and I in mine when the Block Bell rang. Bill shouted to me to answer it, Bill telling me to accept the train being offered which I did.[19]

LNER, like any of the other railway companies, was made up of a multitude of people, a myriad of tiny cogs, each working to ensure that a great machine continued to function. This required the driver's vigilance and the fireman's never-ceasing labours on the swaying foot-plate, as the long train hurtled through the darkness. It required the attentiveness of guards and station staff amidst throngs of passengers and piles of luggage; the

Signalmen operate levers, whilst wearing steel helmets. These, and the steel refuge boxes, were their only protection during air raids. (Public Domain)

precise work of the signalman amid the sharp 'ting' of block bells and clang of levers in the signal box; and above all of the shunter, groping his way in the darkness amid wagons moving down on him from all directions. And then there were the countless men and women in offices, each playing his or her part for ten or twelve hours at a time. There were men and women cleaners in the loco depots and carriage sidings, and there were thousands more at their machines in the workshops. There were the length men who walked the line, in whatever weather came their way, and the men who turned out at all hours to repair what the bombs had wrecked. All these and many more besides played their part, so that the nation could go through to victory. These men and women were the stuff of which a railway is made.

Chapter Three

GREAT WESTERN RAILWAY UNDER ATTACK

Great Western Railway (GWR) linked London with the South West, West and West Midlands of England, and most of Wales. It was founded in 1833, received its enabling act of Parliament on 31 August 1835 and ran its first trains in 1838 with the initial route completed between London and Bristol in 1841. Its most famous engineer was Isambard Kingdom Brunel, who created much of the early infrastructure. GWR was the only company to keep its identity through the Railways Act 1921, which amalgamated it with the remaining independent railways within its territory. GWR was called by some 'God's Wonderful Railway' and by others the 'Great Way Round' but it was also famed as the 'Holiday Line'. This was because it took many people to English and Bristol Channel resorts in the West Country as well as the far South West of England such as Torquay in Devon, Minehead in Somerset, and Newquay and St Ives in Cornwall.

One of the earliest raids in which it suffered was that on Cardiff. On 9 July 1940, the Roath Dock there was attacked for the first time by German bombers. The SS *San Felipe* was badly hit, and six dock workers were trapped in the hold of the ship. For his gallant conduct in rescuing two of them, and recovering the bodies of the other four, John Nicholas Anderson was awarded the British Empire Medal. Anderson was born in Cardiff in 1909 and had worked as a merchant seaman for a short while from

1924, before becoming a dock porter for Great Western Railway. His citation read:

> During an air raid a bomb fell in the hold of a vessel in which six dock labourers were working. Anderson obtained a rope and descended into the hold in which a quantity of timber was burning and smouldering. After the lead had been given by Anderson other helpers followed. In addition to the danger of suffocation from the smoke and fumes they were working under the water line. Two men were rescued alive and sent ashore. Anderson and his fellow rescuers then dug into the burning debris and recovered the bodies of four men who, apparently, had been killed outright by the explosion. Anderson showed initiative and leadership and by his courage set a fine example.[1]

A German intelligence photograph of Roath Dock, Cardiff. (Public Domain)

Perhaps the severest attack in the early part of the Luftwaffe's campaign against the railways occurred at the GWR station in Newton Abbot, Devon. The exact nature of the raid, whether opportunist or planned, remains obscure. If the latter, the reason why a quiet market town nestling below the southern slopes of Dartmoor should have attracted the attention of the Nazi war machine is equally mysterious, but none the less at 18.40 on 20 August 1940 three enemy aircraft approached Torbay and crossed the coast undetected. It was about 18.45, on what had been a fine summer's day when the three enemy aircraft attacked the town with the deliberate intent of bombing the station. A 'yellow' warning had been received that afternoon, which only indicated that enemy aircraft were in the distant vicinity. Railway personnel would normally not seek shelter unless a 'red' warning was received, accompanied by air raid warning sirens. None of this had occurred when the aircraft appeared, flying from east to west and passing over the station and yards at about 200 feet. The raiding force comprised two bombers and a fighter, and the former each dropped five 250kg bombs in the vicinity of the station, whilst the latter strafed the area with machine gun fire. Fortunately the Plymouth-bound passenger express had left the station minutes before the attack began. Six of the bombs which were dropped fell in the station and yards. One struck a rail in a carriage siding and failed to explode, coming to rest just two roads away from a 'King' No. 6010. It was not discovered until three quarters of an hour after the raid. Bomb disposal teams immediately set to work, but it was not made safe until the following morning, resulting in a delay of some ten hours whilst all traffic in the immediate area was halted.

Of the five bombs which did explode, one fell between the down through road and the adjacent carriage siding. This was closely followed by the second which fell some 8 feet away on the down relief line itself. These two bombs were responsible for most of the damage sustained and the majority of the human casualties suffered during the raid. Large portions of the down through and down relief lines were wrecked and extensive damage was caused to the nearby carriage sidings. The island platform serving the down relief line and the down main line was in part demolished, causing extensive damage to the refreshment room, general waiting room, bookstall and both ladies and gents' toilets. The tobacconist's kiosk was completely destroyed, and extensive damage was caused to the platform roof for most of its length.

Standing on the down main line at the time of the attack was the 19.00 ex-Newton Abbot local stopper to Plymouth. The train had been partially shielded from the blast by the station buildings, but this did not prevent it from sustaining substantial damage and loss of life. The first coach, a brake third (No. 4941) was so seriously damaged that half of it had been completely blown away. Incredibly, the frame had not suffered to any great extent, and a small terrier dog which had been stowed in the luggage compartment was rescued unharmed. Near the demolished tobacconist's kiosk, a length of rail measuring over 44 feet in length had been blown up onto the roof. Three other rails of similar length were blown out of the station completely,

Damage at Newton Abbott station following the German raid. (Public Domain)

one of them landing in a nearby park, some 150 yards away. Another landed 200 yards distant and the third came down in the road outside the station. A line of six coaches in the second carriage siding suffered the full blast of the first two bombs, and sustained great damage. Another line of five carriages in the first carriage siding also suffered severe damage and two carriage cleaners and a gas fitter who were working near this rolling stock were killed.

A third bomb fell on to the junction of the lines leading to the coaling stage, destroying a wall and rupturing a water main, which then proceeded to flood the resulting crater. Just over 40 feet away stood another engine, No. 6010 *King Charles I* which having had a near miss with the bomb which did not explode, received slight damage from the second. Further damage was sustained when the German fighter proceeded to shoot up the station with machine gun fire and No. 6010 was hit numerous times. Most of the bullet holes were in the tender, which one eye witness later described as looking 'like a prairie wagon after an attack by Indians'. Driver Palmer and fireman French who were aboard at the time were both injured.

At 100 feet nearer the coaling stage, the fourth bomb hit the number one pit road, close to 0-6-0 pannier tank No. 2785. The little engine was the worst mechanical casualty of the raid, suffering severe damage, and was later cut up in situ. It had suffered a broken frame, two broken wheels and had its side rods twisted out of all recognition. Its right-hand water tank was blown off its mountings and was severely punctured. The fact that this engine took the full brunt of the blast from the bomb probably saved the life of fire dropper Hitt who was working on No. 6801 *Aylburton Grange* just beyond it. He escaped without injury, even though this bomb, like the others, lifted several 44-foot lengths of rail over his engine and deposited them in a field 150 yards away.

In the same vicinity, but 90 feet nearer the coaling stage fell the fifth bomb which again exploded near the number one pit road.

Five other locomotives were in this vicinity, grouped together, these being No. 6801, with No. 5915 *Trentham Hall* immediately behind. Three roads away was 2-6-2 tank engine No. 3180, directly in the line of the blast, with 0-6-0 tender No. 8353 some distance behind, whilst another similar tender No. 9311 was one road away. *Trentham Hall* was partially protected by a line of ash wagons but this did not save it from having its chimney blown off and its tender holed. The ash wagons were derailed and two were virtually demolished, with their cargo of ash scattered over a wide area. *Aylburton Grange* was derailed and struck by flying debris, whilst No. 9311 was more seriously damaged. Its cab, firebox and tender were peppered with shrapnel holes. Whilst the outside casing of the firebox was penetrated, the copper plating was only bulged. The rear driving wheel was punctured on the rim and in the counter balance weight. The rear end of the frame and the bottom of the cab were also twisted. Nos. 8353 and 3180 were mainly hit by soft debris and damage was mainly confined to broken windows. Driver Tozer and fireman Wilfred Gilpin who were aboard the latter suffered minor injuries, and were lucky not to have been killed as their engine was within the lethal range of both the fourth and fifth bombs.

The nearby wagon shop was the scene of great drama, as one of the bombs lifted another 44-foot length of rail into the air above it, so high indeed that it came down end first and pieced the roof vertically. It continued its downward trajectory through the body of a goods wagon inside, smashing a wheel off and pushing it forward some 6 feet. Assistant foreman Francis Fenning and wagon repairer Sydney Hoyle who were sheltering beneath it had a miraculous escape, for both could easily have been crushed. It is worth remembering that, despite the number of such instances where fate intervened to spare individuals from the expected results of high explosive detonations, this was a comparatively small raid. In common with the press nationally at this time, which was under heavy government censorship, details published in the local papers afterwards about the incident were extremely sketchy, the only damage reported being that to a row of cottages. No mention was made of the damage to the railway line or goods shed, lest that information might find its way back to the enemy. A further boost to civilian morale was given by the statement in the report that two of the attackers were shot down by fighters from the RAF, a detail which appears to be entirely fictitious given the fact that the alert status was still at 'yellow' when the enemy aircraft left. In addition to those civilians who were killed, more than sixty were injured.

Birmingham was the scene of more bravery when at Bordesley Junction on 26–27 August 1940, an 18-year-old GWR locomotive cleaner, driving a railway engine for the first time in his life, moved a number of loaded wagons from the side of a blazing shed. Perhaps unsurprisingly, Peter Frederick Smout from Acock's Green was from a railway family – his father was an engine driver. After the incident, Smout recalled:

> We heard a funny noise outside. Opening the door I saw incendiaries in the yard. We all did our best to get these out; then I went over the other side of the yard, where a fire had started. Mr Clarke, the yardmaster's clerk, said to me, 'Can you drive an engine?' I replied, 'I'll do my best,' and got on the engine. There wasn't enough steam to pull out the wagons at one go, so I pulled out half, then pulled out the other half. I kept inside the cab. It was fairly warm, but that kept the majority of the heat off.[2]

Smout was awarded the George Medal, as was Frederick Francis Blake, an engine cleaner who showed little regard for his own safety during the same incident. Noticing a wagon on fire, Blake with assistance propelled it by hand to a place of safety. After doing this, Blake went to an air raid shelter, enlisted the help of the men therein and organised a squad to move other burning trucks. He also acted as shunter to Smout, and operated the point lever, which had become very hot, by using his cap. Afterwards

Blake put out a number of incendiaries, using both his hands and his feet to cover them in ballast. Subsequently he found a stirrup pump, with which he extinguished the fires on several other trucks. Mr J.E. Clark the yardmaster's clerk, received the OBE for his work in also organising volunteer squads to remove wagons and extinguish fires, again with little regard for his own safety.

In the autumn of 1940, Bill Morgan was a GWR passed fireman, working out of Neyland terminal in South Wales. At this time of year daylight faded early, and it was soon time to fix the 'sails' as the canvas cab cover was known. This was a contraction of 'Zeppelin sails' as they were known in the First World War. (As a point of detail, it had initially been thought that seven different designs of canvas tarpaulins would be sufficient to cover all types of engine used by the GWR. Eventually, however, no fewer than forty-five different designs were listed by the company's Swindon drawing office.) On 1 September, the station at Neyland had already been on yellow alert when driver Freddie Enyon and Morgan arrived to book on that afternoon. Instead of the usual Castle awaiting them, there was a 53 class loco. The Castles arrived here in the morning with the down parcels, and were made ready for the return run with the up parcels in the afternoon. However, wartime emergencies and shortages of men meant that there were often irregularities, hence the 53 class that they found themselves with that particular day.

With a yellow alert in place it was necessary to cover the glare from the firebox, even though it was merely dusk. Morgan hooked up the rear of the sail to the metal uprights attached to the front of the tender for this purpose, while Enyon threw back the side flaps onto the top. They generally avoided fastening these down until absolutely necessary, as the footplate quickly became unbearably hot when fully closed in. After carrying out all the standard checks Morgan stood and looked, with some misgivings, at the centre and sidelights which denoted the fact that they were a parcel train. These threw two penetrating beams of light forward, which also of course increased the possibility of their being spotted by an enemy aircraft. This was particularly concerning in a red alert situation, especially if it happened to be an ammunition train that they were driving! To Morgan it seemed ludicrous to take such stringent measures over the blacking out of stations and fitting of sails to cabs, only to then advertise the location of the trains with blazing headlights.

Each of these lights had a bulls-eye reflector which concentrated the light into a beam which shone out ahead of the train. A slit was positioned behind the front plate of glass where red or green slides could be fitted in order to change the purpose of the light, and so many firemen and drivers started to place a slip of white paper into this slit, which reduced the strength of the bullseye and diffused the light. Although this brought some comfort to the train crews concerned, as soon as this practice came to the attention of management it was decreed that it was illegal, and that disciplinary action would follow any discovery of lights which had been tampered with in such a fashion. So they were forced to return to the original situation of blazing lights cutting through the otherwise blacked-out countryside. Some crews tried turning down the wick, in order to reduce the strength of the lamp, but on a rough stretch of track this would inevitably cause the lamp to go out altogether, resulting in the train being halted by a signalman due to absence of lights. Others tried turning up the wick further in the hope that in burning more fiercely, it would blacken the glass. This also had little effect, so it was a case of back to square one. Only when pulling an ammunition train did Morgan put personal preservation first, and defy the order.

On this particular run, with the 53 class, there were only innocuous parcels aboard, so the two men agreed that they had better abide by the rules. Thus they set off into the dusk with their two headlamps blazing, and side sails firmly secured to the cab. As they passed through cuttings and countryside into the darkening night, fireman Morgan grew increasingly hot and sweaty as he shovelled coal into the firebox. The situation to him seemed as ridiculous as ever. Using sails fixed down was bad enough, but driver Enyon soon became aware of another problem as a drop of water landed on the back of his neck – the engine had a leaky valve. Even without this the condensation would soon start to form on the inside of the sails, but with the faulty valve the interior of the cab soon began to feel like a tropical rainforest, the humidity sapping the crew of all energy. In a state of misery, with sweat pouring off him, Morgan closed the firebox door and opened the side-sails to try to dry out the atmosphere inside, and blow some fresh air in to allow them to breathe more easily. However the unintended consequence was also a sudden drop in temperature. From the steamy jungles of Africa, the cab reverted to the conditions at one of the Poles in a matter of seconds. Neither option was pleasant, but there seemed to be no happy medium, so they continued their run to Llandeilo Junction with the top valve of the pet-pipe hissing all the way in spite of their attempts to bind it up. They reverted to jungle conditions, the condensation dripping relentlessly all over them, and to make matters worse by the time they reached Llandeilo Junction the yellow alert had changed to red.

They had a strong suspicion that Swansea would be the target that night, but there was also the possibility that they would be caught up in the attack. Standing alongside the track drinking a refreshing cup of tea, they first became aware of the drone of high-flying aircraft. As they strained their eyes looking up into the dark night sky they gradually became aware of the white outlines of parachutes – each one carrying a burning flare as it slowly descended. Handing the driver his cup of tea for a second, Morgan told him to look away as matters would not then concern him later. He took two pieces of paper from his double-home box and fitted them to the lamps at the front of the train. With trouble likely to be ahead, he now felt safer. As they steamed away from Llandeilo Junction the flares continued to light up the sky ahead, and more ominously the sound of bombs exploding could now also plainly be heard. The sails were now well down as the train rattled along, but the build-up of heat and humidity inside was less of a concern now as their attention was focused solely upon the danger from the skies above them.

Thankfully they were now approaching Llandarcy Tunnel, which offered a degree of sanctuary if only for a few minutes. Inside, they would be unseen and protected from bombs, if only for a short time. Their speed would be restricted passing through the tunnel, as there was a signal just beyond it. It was always off, but this time, to their dismay, for the first time it was on. Reacting quickly Fred slowed them down just outside the tunnel – the signal was about 75 yards further on. The driver quickly assessed the situation and decided that there was no sense in waiting outside the tunnel; they would be safer inside and so he reversed the few yards back, to await the signal indicating that they had the road.

The view out of the tunnel was restricted by the steep sides of the cutting, but in the distance the horizon was aglow with fires which lit up the night sky, revealing more parachute flares falling ahead of them. Now and again the loco shuddered as a bomb exploded nearby; some were so close that the blast was deafening. Morgan pointed out that if this kind of destruction went on for much longer there would be no signal left for them to observe. Under Rule 55 of GWR, having waited the regulation three minutes, one of them should have approached the signal box to ascertain the cause of the delay, and to check that they were properly guarded. However, on this occasion the reason for the delay was clearly obvious in front of them. Morgan none the less volunteered to go and check, as soon as there was any lift in the bombing. Before he could do so he was forced to duck involuntarily by the scream of a particularly close bomb, which was followed by an explosion and the tinkling of thousands of pieces of glass – the sound of a signal box taking a direct hit.

Morgan climbed down from the footplate and made his way to the entrance to the tunnel, squeezing past the boiler of the 53 class and out into the night. Searchlights swept the sky, directing the fire of anti-aircraft guns, and the drone of aircraft was still prevalent overhead. Covering his arms with his head he ran on up the track, past the signal which was still on, until a flash illuminated the signal box, still standing, about 100 yards further on. He hurried forward until he reached the steps – looking up, the box which towered over him stood deserted and in darkness, every pane of glass having been blown out by a near miss. Racing up the steps he pushed open the door and forced his way into the draughty darkened box, all the while broken glass was crunching under his feet. He called out, but there was no answer. Why would a signalman desert his post? Suddenly the glare of a falling flare provided the answer. In the corner stood a metal box, 6 foot high and 3 feet square – the signalman's shelter. As he heaved open the door a startled face looked back at him. Sitting down reading a book by torchlight, the signalman looked for all the world as if he was sitting on the lavatory. He was not best pleased at the intrusion, and told Morgan so. When he showed no sign of leaving his reading matter, Morgan asked what he was supposed to do, he answered testily that as all communications were down, he should obey the signal and wait it out in the safety of the tunnel – just like he was doing. Morgan could not decide if the signalman was incredibly brave or incredibly stupid. Either way, it must have been a damned good book.

Picking his way back through the debris, Morgan returned to the safety of the tunnel where Fred was anxiously awaiting news of what was going on with the box. They waited there for nearly two hours until gradually the explosions became fewer, though the glow on the horizon remained fiercely red. The guard meanwhile had come up from his van at the back of the train to wait at the engine with the others. Suddenly he noticed that the signal was off, and pointed it out to the driver and fireman before hurrying back to his post as the train prepared to move away. As they crept warily out of the tunnel, they saw the signalman ahead, now waving a red light backwards and forwards, so Fred halted the train beside the shattered signal box. The signalman told them exactly what they already knew – communications were still out, and as there might be debris on the line, it was necessary to proceed with caution. As they passed by, he waved to the guard and was last seen climbing the rickety steps to his signal box.

After a slow journey at 5mph, they eventually arrived at Briton Ferry. Surprisingly there was no debris on the track, though dark gaping craters could be seen in the fields beside the line. Now they found that the target had not been Swansea as they assumed, but Llandarcy with its oil storage tanks. They found they could go no further with the parcel train and were told to leave the 53 class at Briton Ferry. They waited in the cabin drinking tea with five others, all of them waiting to get to Landore, so it was decided to take a light engine down and they could all stand on the footplate. It was crowded, but no one seemed to mind, even though the speed restrictions in place made the journey interminable. Nearing Landore, fires were still burning and occasional explosions could still be heard from the oil tanks. The driver on this stretch was a local Swansea man who knew every inch of the track. He halted the engine just before the iron bridge outside Landore and instructed one of the others to go on ahead and check the state of it. The man walked slowly over, examining the track and checking underneath to see if the supports were intact. With no obvious damage they proceeded but no one said a word until the engine was safely on the other side. By the time they reached Landore another wave of bombers had arrived, and they had to run through the deserted streets to reach their lodgings at 01.00. At 06.00 after the all clear had sounded they made their way to Swansea station, but such was the general state of confusion that their passenger train did not run, and they made their way back to Neyland as passengers on a mail train.

When the Nazi raids on London began in earnest, the stations and depots of Paddington (the main GWR terminus in the capital) were an obvious target. Flares were constantly dropped over the Paddington-Westbourne Park area, and many sticks of high explosive bombs, clearly intended for the railway and for those who worked on it, were dropped in nearby streets. They smashed and destroyed civilian homes and commercial property alike. However, the ARP organisation at Paddington station was not called into action until September 1940, but from then on incidents were more or less constant. From 11 September until the end of December they dealt with 144 incendiary bombs, 12 high explosive bombs, 2 oil bombs and 3 delayed-action bombs. Almost invariably the havoc caused, by whatever type of device, was considerable but at the same time it was met with coolness and composure.

In fact, only twelve high explosive bombs actually fell on Great Western property (or close enough to damage it) up to the end of December 1940. In the same time period thirty-eight high explosives and innumerable incendiaries landed near enough to Paddington to be deemed 'near misses'. After a while, such incidents were almost considered 'routine' by railway staff. Although anti-aircraft fire had been heard in the vicinity in late August, and some bombs were dropped in the Paddington district, the first to actually hit the railway fell at approximately 00.37 on 11 September; a string of incendiaries was dropped by a German bomber flying diagonally across the railway from the direction of Westbourne Park Villas. Nine of these hit the railway, and the remaining three fell near the Lords Hill shunters cabin. The goods warden at once made a report to ARP headquarters, and the goods fire squad soon appeared, but in the meantime the shunters and two engine men got on with the job on their own and fought the fires themselves. So effective were they that all the bombs were extinguished within five minutes of landing.

Another incendiary landed on the Horse Sanatorium in the Old Mileage Yard at Westbourne Park, and another damaged the main petrol pump at the Alfred Road Garage. The first of these was promptly dealt with by a railway carman and a local fire warden, and the bomb at the garage was also quickly dealt with. This particular raid was noticeable for the substantial increase in British anti-aircraft fire which met the enemy force. Up to that point, anti-aircraft fire had been derisory and disappointing, but the roar of fire that night was described as deafening. It gave much heart to the civilians, as Prime Minister Winston Churchill recognised, even if it was somewhat ineffective. During that month of September, the government was deeply concerned about the fall in industrial output because of the repeated aerial bombardment of cities. It was the custom of many factories for the staff to take to the shelters the moment that an air raid siren went off, and that wardens started blowing whistles. It was not however the case with railway staff. People could – and did – blow whistles at them, but to the lasting credit of all railwaymen they went into a shelter only if directly attacked, and even then many of them remained at their posts. An official report stated: 'It is not on record that any anxiety was felt in Government circles so far as the conduct of the railwaymen during the air raids was concerned.'[3]

Though bombs might be bursting on the track and on the sidings, it was a matter of pride that the trains had to keep on running. In a terse statement unburdened by unnecessary rhetoric, the general manager of the GWR decreed that:

> During Air Raids it is essential that both Passenger and Freight trains should continue to run as required. Train-men and signal-men should remain at their posts. All other staff should continue to work during Air Raids until danger is imminent in the immediate vicinity of the place at which they are working. The staff should resume work as soon as the immediate danger is passed.[4]

Be that as it may, the dislocation caused by air attacks meant that timetables were completely disrupted during this period. GWR fireman Fred Simpson remembered the hours spent waiting on the track in sidings and loops miles from anywhere, due to interruptions in service through enemy bombing:

> I remembering being in a loop at Knighton Crossing once. Six trains were held there. Eventually we had to leave the train and go home, and we came back twelve hours later to take over the same train! It often took as much as twenty-three hours to get from Swindon to Reading during the war. We'd sit there in the dark on the footplate for hours with nothing to do and – worse – nothing to eat or drink. Then when we had to work it back it would take three quarters of an hour![5]

If they were stopped at a country signal, miles from anywhere the footplatemen would curse their luck, but sometimes things were not quite as bad:

> We used to get stopped for ages every now and then at a signal near where an aunt of mine lived. More than once we dashed off to her house for a fry-up. And at another signal there was a pub nearby – I think that the men used to pray that if they were going to be held up it would be at that signal! Mind you, I did hear that, what with the war being on, as often as not they got to the pub only to find that they had run out of beer![6]

At 21.10 on 24 September, heavy explosions rocked Paddington station. Shortly afterwards reports were received that one high explosive bomb had fallen in the passenger yard, destroying the shunters' cabin. By sheer chance it was unoccupied at the time, but the bomb had also damaged the up main and relief lines. A first aid team rushed to the scene, but the total casualties amounted to an engineman who was suffering from shock and a traveller who was cut by glass. They were followed by an engineering squad who worked through the night to get the lines open to traffic once again. That same night another bomb struck the canal wharf in the Harrow Road, behind the goods station. Serious damage was done to windows, and a fire telephone in the shed was blown out of its cabinet, thus sounding the alarm at the fire station all by itself. The trailer pump team duly turned out, but reaching the scene of the incident discovered that they were not required.

Two days later on 26 September incendiaries littered the mileage yards at 01.15, but the fires were tackled by a combination of the Great Western Fire Brigade, Metropolitan Police, and the AFS. Coal wharves and a few vehicles were damaged, but that was all. About the same time a solitary incendiary struck a coach of the empty 00.10 arrival train, but was extinguished by the train staff. The same night Paddington again received the attention of the enemy. At 22.47 incendiaries scattered across the station, with one falling on platform 1, two falling on the roof of the Royal Hotel, and others reaching the Mint Stables and arrival and departure roadways. When dawn came, one unexploded device was found resting between the rails of platform 9's track, having failed to ignite.

The worst was yet to come however, and the night of 13 October would see numerous gallant actions performed, many of these by the men and women of the first aid staff. At about 23.23 three large high explosive bombs came down in the middle of Praed Street, adjoining the Royal Hotel. One of the bombs burst on the Praed Street Inner Circle station, where, as usual there was a crowd of travellers waiting on the platform. Six of the passengers were killed outright and a number were injured. Within a few seconds of the bombs exploding, every available man and woman of the first aid parties was at work tending to the wounded. The platforms of the station were scenes of devastation; everywhere there was shattered masonry and twisted metalwork, broken glass and splintered wood. Visibility was already poor owing to blackout restrictions, but that night conditions were made a hundred times worse by the clouds of dust which filled the subway leading to the big station. The dust choked the rescuers, and they could hardly breathe as they went about their vital work. Debris was still coming down as they arrived, and they were in grave danger from precarious masonry and metalwork, but the cries of the wounded could not be ignored, and the rescuers never faltered for an instant.

Led by the deputy principal first aid warden, the men and women of the party went headlong into the chaos, and though half blinded by smoke and dust, got to work at once. They first of all sorted out those who had been killed and covered them up. Then they took them away out of sight. The more serious cases – in some instances involving the loss of an arm or leg or both – were identified and given immediate aid. In an astonishingly short space of time, they were on their way to hospital. There were so many injured that the ambulances which had arrived were not sufficient to take them all, and every sort of available vehicle was commandeered for use as an emergency ambulance. The police, off duty servicemen and railway staff all acted as stretcher bearers. By 23.50 all the urgent cases had been dealt with at the railway casualty clearing station under the care of the medical officer in charge, and sent off to hospital. Many of those who were injured that night later wrote letters of thanks expressing their appreciation of the care that they received in the aftermath of the bombing.

During October 1940, the marshalling yards in the vicinity of London experienced an 'alert' almost every night, with the result that out of 382 hours of night, shunting had to be carried out on complete darkness for 299 of them. Although Alfred Summers' duties as a fireman did not take him on shunting turns, he was on turns that brought trains into Old Oak Common yard. Old Oak Common and Willesden (LMS) sheds, as well as the nearby Park Royal industrial estate were all prime targets for Hitler's bombers, but whilst the other facilities received hits on several occasions, Old Oak Common seemed to lead a charmed life, at least to begin with. This was perhaps due to the anti-aircraft batteries which were situated close by on Wormwood Scrubs, but

Great Western Railway Fireman Alfred Summers. (A.W. Summers)

the presumed immunity of the depot would soon come to a spectacular end.

One day Summers was returning with his driver on a 5700 class pannier tank and a train of loaded box vans from South Lambeth. They had just crossed the LMS line at North Pole Junction on to their own line and had proceeded alongside the down main line to the reception line in the shunting sidings, where they came to a halt. All seemed strangely quiet – the guns on Wormwood Scrubs were silent, the clock on the carriage department offices read 13.23, the driver was making some entries in his daily record and shunting was in progress all around. Then, slowly but clearly, the noise of a Spitfire's Merlin engine could be heard growing louder. This familiar and friendly sound at first drew no attention, but then, from somewhere behind came the unmistakable chilling whistle of a falling bomb. There was no time to move or do anything but listen for the explosion. There followed a terrific blast which seemed to lift the engine momentarily off the rails. One after another came more bombs, followed each time by a huge explosion. About eight bombs in total were dropped, and the second which landed behind the engine (and left a huge crater in the track) once again lifted the locomotive into the air momentarily.

A third bomb somehow missed all the main lines, but hit the roof of the carriage department offices. The clock topped at 13.25 and was to remain stuck at that time for some years afterwards! Had the building been hit twenty-five minutes later, about sixty of the staff of the carriage sidings would have been in their cabins, changing out of their overalls to go off duty. There could be little doubt that all of them would have been killed, but as it was, the only casualty was a burst water main which never the less caused considerable disruption through flooding. A fourth bomb hit the locomotive paint shop and demolished it, while the sixth, seventh and eighth, no doubt intended for the locomotive shed, all missed. One narrowly missed the Grand Union Canal wall, which ran alongside the building and had this been breached, hundreds of tons of water would have poured into the shed. All this took place in a very narrow window of time, during which not one anti-aircraft gun fired a shot.

Like everyone else, the gunners were taken completely by surprise, being deceived by the sound of the aircraft engines. Considerable chaos was caused but for Summers the biggest concern was that although most of the bombs had missed their intended targets, some might have fallen on nearby All Souls Avenue where his wife was living at the time. Fortunately, he got home to find that the house had been spared. However, the strain of such events was terrific, both for the railwaymen who were worried about their families, and for the families themselves who were often spending night after night sheltering from bombing in Underground stations. Shortly after Christmas 1940, Summers and a number of other drivers and firemen at Old Oak Common who had families would apply for transfers out of London. Summers would apply (and be accepted) for a position at Didcot locomotive shed, a small depot 17 miles beyond Reading. Although it would mean that, as a footplateman, he would still be exposed to danger, at least he would have the peace of mind of knowing that his wife and son were both safe.

One November night at 00.15 a high explosive bomb struck the line only 10 yards from the signal box operated by Charles Dearden Stickley. He had been in the service of the railway company for thirty-two years and for the last ten had been on duty in that self-same signal box, so it was no surprise that he knew it inside out and backwards. The longest period he had previously been under attack had begun one Sunday at 17.37 and went on continuously until 08.00 the following morning. He had on that occasion endured twelve hours in semi-darkness, with all communication with the outside world cut off. Back then a bomb had fallen behind his box, yet his greatest fear was not for himself, but for his family at West Ealing who were also caught up in the raid. Now, the force of the explosion tore out all the underneath part of the box, and all points as far as Ealing were blasted. Next came a series of incendiaries and all the lights in the box went out. For two hours Stickley was entirely alone, with a series of damaged points requiring repair. Stickley continues: 'But then Mr Honeybone came along on his bicycle. We had 57 consecutive nights of blitz. Each night Mr Honeybone was on duty ... and we all knew he would turn up sooner or later ... to see that we were all right and to lend a hand if we were not.'[7]

Frederick Honeybone, aged 50, was one of GWR's district inspectors, covering the London district, under a divisional superintendent who had 5,200 railwaymen under his command. The district inspectors knew all the men in their district personally. They knew their temperament, their personality, their family circumstances and were at one and the same time guides, philosophers and friends. To have such a mentor was all the more important for signalmen under the strain of war.

Other less serious incidents occurred that autumn. On 6 November at 18.55, a high explosive bomb hit the Royal Oak station – just outside of Paddington on Lord Hill's Bridge – where three coaches and a line were damaged. The down Metropolitan line was also wrecked here, and the waiting room was destroyed. A few days later on the night of 12 November, a large bomb landed among motor lorries and carts which were parked in the goods station yard. Four of these vehicles were destroyed, whilst eighteen were badly damaged and twenty-three suffered less serious knocks and scratches. One cart was blown clean over the boundary wall and out of the yard, to find a watery grave

Frederick Dainty Cox, awarded the George Medal for removing an unexploded bomb. (Author's Collection)

in the nearby Grand Union Canal. Fortunately, there were no human casualties in this incident.

Away from London, a Great Western employee, Frederick Dainty Cox, whose home was at 8 Queen Street, Lydney, Gloucestershire, was to be awarded the George Medal for bravery following a German raid on 9 November 1940. The target of the raid was the Woolaston and Beachley Junction, near Gloucester. The official announcement in *The London Gazette* read as follows:

> Frederick Dainty Cox, telegraph linesman's assistant, Great Western Railway. Immediately after an enemy raid, it was found that railway communications had been broken and Cox and another railwayman were sent to examine the line. It was found that one bomb had exploded and broken several telegraph wires, whilst an unexploded time bomb had fallen on the permanent way. After repairing the most important of the damaged telegraph circuits, Cox carried the bomb to the down side of the line and dropped it over the boundary hedge on to soft ground. This enabled a single line to be put into operation. Although warned by the police to stop work, as another time bomb had been dropped nearby, both men continued until repairs to the wires had been completed. Cox then searched for and found the second bomb and helped the Bomb Disposal staff to move it to a place of safety.[8]

When first informed of the honour that had been conferred upon him, and in reply to congratulations extended to him, Cox very modestly replied:

> 'It was nothing. I only did my duty.' In the course of further conversation, Mr. Cox revealed the fact that he was working for three hours on the telegraph lines before he had time to remove the bomb. With smile, Mr. Cox said he intended to have little celebration tonight. Mr. Cox, who is 38 years of age is a married man with three children.[9]

Later after his investiture at Buckingham Palace, Cox is reported as saying: 'I expected it would be a terrible ordeal, but there was a delightful lack of formality and I enjoyed it very much.'[10]

Back at Paddington there then followed a period of calm for a few weeks, in which the most dramatic incident was when a barrage balloon broke free of its moorings, and trailed its cable across the live rails between the passenger and goods stations, the ensuing attempts to recapture it providing much needed light relief to all who watched them. Matters became serious once again on 3 December when a large delayed-action bomb fell near the road transport depot at Alfred Road. The entire depot had to be evacuated, and the staff were not able to get back to work there until 8 December, when the bomb disposal squad at last succeeded, after repeated attempts, in dealing with this unwelcome visitor.

GWR, like all the railway companies, was taken over by the government immediately war was declared, and it was soon a regular occurrence to see all sorts of unusual locomotives, particularly in the London area, working on jobs previously the preserve of some other type of engine. As an example of this, the 5700 class 0-6-0 condensing tanks, Nos. 9700 to 9710, had always been used exclusively for conveying meat, in refrigerated containers, from Acton yard to Paddington suburban, and thence to Smithfield Meat Market via the Underground lines.

These engines had a pipe from the smokebox to the water tank and the fireman, by operating a lever at his side known as the 'chopper' could condense the smoke and exhaust steam in the water tank, thus ensuring that no smoke was emitted into the Underground tunnels. These condensing locomotives were now appearing on other work, to release more suitable engines for heavier traffic.

Summers remembered an incident at Didcot when a senior passenger driver, who had been assigned to take one of these engines of this class back to Old Oak Common, was confused by it, despite his extensive experience. Summers was preparing his own engine, when he heard this man ask his fireman, who was standing on top of the locomotive with the bag of the water-column in the tank, in forceful terms how much more 'ruddy water' it wanted. Meekly, the fireman replied that it was just over a foot from the top of the tank. From where Summers was standing, he could see that water was pouring from the tank overflow pipe. It was evident that neither fireman nor driver knew that it was not possible to fill the water tank right up to the top on these locomotives, as a space was left above the water level to condense the smoke from the boiler when working on the London Transport Underground lines to Smithfield. Another concession to wartime conditions was the variation in quality of fuel. Great Western engines were built especially to burn South Wales anthracite, which was excellent coal. Although they were deliberately engineered for this particular fuel, in wartime this might be substituted for Darlton Main, which was also good steam coal; 'Yorkshire Hard' as it was also known generally made for a very clean fire. The worst coal was that cut from the Wigan area. In peacetime as a general rule freight trains did not get good coal. That was kept for passenger trains, in particular the expresses, but in wartime it was often a case of using what was available. Generally, across the rail network it was felt that although operationally GWR had a reputation for slackness, they none the less had great engines.

A cartoon from a national newspaper shows a train loaded with war materiel passing a cheery businessman. In fact, the additional strain imposed by war work had a detrimental effect on passenger services. (Author's Collection)

Another rare sight in the London division were the Aberdare double framed 2-6-0, used entirely on freight working and which usually remained in the South Wales area. These engines, which some claim to have been the worst ever built by GWR, were now becoming an increasingly common sight between Swindon and Acton yard. Coal trains such as these were given little preference on the main lines, and drivers found now that they were often turned onto loops to allow government munitions or sometimes troop trains to pass. Passenger traffic had also been reduced, in order to free up engines for this essential work. Drivers and firemen were exempted from joining the forces, as it was felt that their specialised experience of train working was a more effective contribution to the war effort than serving on the front line. Never the less, problems arose, with the appearance of fit young men in civilian clothes likely to provoke the ire of mothers whose own sons had been conscripted into the forces. Therefore, it became necessary to issue railwaymen with badges to identify them as war workers. As time went on, however, less skilled railwaymen were called up, and it became increasingly common to see women guards, ticket collectors and even permanent way workers. Harold Gasson was a young cleaner at Didcot Loco Depot, and remembered:

> Cleaning engines in 1941 with the War well and truly on became very much a secondary occupation, and we Cleaners were pressed into covering every job in the Shed. There was an acute shortage of labour in those days, so we washed out boilers acting as boilersmith mates, assisted the fitters as mates, dropped fires, and coaled engines, but it was all good training in the running of a busy locomotive shed. One job we all hated was coaling engines, as it meant shovelling coal out of a 20 ton wagon into tubs, then tipping the contents of the tub into the tender waiting below. It always seemed to me that whenever I was detailed to work at the coal stage it was blowing a gale; consequently one was covered with coal dust in the first hour. One task that gave light relief was damping down fires on the ash road. This was necessary because the glow of dropped fires during the night gave away the position of the Shed to German bombers, so a Cleaner was detailed to use a hose pipe to damp down the glowing coals as the firebox was being emptied … A cold dismal morning in early February of 1941 found me in the fire-box of 5935 Norton Hall equipped with flare lamp, short pricker,

> and handbrush. It was not such a bad place to be as she still had 40lbs showing on the steam gauge and was pleasantly warm. She was booked in for washout and tubes, so my task was to hook the 'corks' of clinker out of the tubeplate, then brush off the brick-arch. At 7.00am I was well on my way to completion when I heard banging on the steel footplate and my name being called. I stood up, with my head and shoulders sticking out of the firebox doors to see the shift Foreman, Jack Jacobs, calling me. He informed me that the Fireman on the West End Pilot had gone home sick and I would have to take over the duty. I quickly climbed out of the firebox, handed in my tools to the Chargehand Cleaner, picked up my box from the Cleaners' cabin and made my way to Didcot West End Box … The duty was booked until 2.00pm so this would be my first turn as a Fireman.[11]

At Old Oak Common the glass roof of the shed had naturally been blacked over, but drivers and firemen were still compelled to

A Great Western Railway war service badge. (Author's Collection)

have the engine blackout sheets down all round when preparing a locomotive for the road at night. Whilst the blackout sheets prevented the light from the fire escaping, they also trapped heat inside, and the crews would sweat profusely in the humid atmosphere within, even on cold winter nights; at times it was almost too much for them to bear. In these blackout conditions, taking on water at the columns in winter was a miserable job. The water that dripped from the bag after the previous use would freeze round the column and, because the ice could not be seen in the darkness, firemen very often slipped over on it; many times also the air raid sirens would begin to wail to add to the discomfort. Summers remembered:

> When this happened we were inclined to go to the air raid shelters, until we realised that this was a great help to Hitler and just what he would like to happen, because once the railway ceased to run, Britain would come to a halt. We knew that the main targets of the Luftwaffe would be the locomotive sheds and freight yards, but this was our war effort and, although we were in a reserved occupation, this really was the front line as much as any in France.[12]

Engine crews had been issued with gas masks and steel helmets, which they were required to carry at all times although he recalled that they did not need orders to carry them; during air raids shrapnel often fell like red hot rain, and on two occasions he had to dive for cover as low-flying enemy aircraft machine-gunned the shed as he was walking towards the coal stage. Another typical incident concerned a government stores train that they were bringing in from Wolverhampton:

> It had been a nightmare journey all the way, especially through the industrial area of Birmingham, and as we approached Snow Hill Tunnel we felt sure that we were never going to get through. As far as lighting the streets

> was concerned, Birmingham should have been completely blacked out, but the power of the flares and incendiary bombs dropped by the German planes, despite the terrific hammering they were getting from the anti-aircraft guns, lit up everything as if it were daylight. Coming out of Snow Hill Tunnel we quickly took in our signals, which were at 'line clear.' My driver and I breathed a sigh of relief because at last, it seemed that we could still keep going. Once through Tyseley we began to leave the factory area behind, but on both sides of the line, bombs that were undoubtedly meant for the railway were falling everywhere. Fortunately we had a very free steaming 'Hall', and despite the fact that my driver and I were working completely covered in by the black out sheets I was able to keep a full head of steam.
>
> Solihull was quickly passed, and approaching Lapworth, all that could be heard was the bark of the engine's exhaust. After passing through Hatton and Warwick we swept round the bend which brought us into Leamington, where we knew we would be stopped if, for any reason, we could not proceed. Here we stopped to take water, and took the opportunity to ask the station staff about the situation ahead. We were informed that everything was quiet as far as Oxford. We were soon under way again, and after passing Fenny Compton my driver shut off steam. I shut the Firehole doors, and took down the black-out sheets to get a welcome breath of fresh air.[13]

From here, they could maintain speed on to Banbury without additional coal being required on the fire. At Banbury, it was possible for them to hear but not see shunting in progress, whilst faint glimmers of light were visible from beneath engines standing in the shed. Oxford was passed without incident as was Didcot, but at Reading they were stopped at the West Junction signal box and told by the signalman that there was an 'air raid red', code words which meant that London was being bombed again. As if to confirm that this was indeed the case, the sky in the distance was glowing crimson. These 'air raid red' warnings were actually quite common, being a nightly occurrence in the most intense period of the Battle for the Railways. On another occasion, with a 6300 class 2-6-0, Summers and his driver received the usual warnings approaching the capital and by Slough the bombing and gunfire could be heard plainly. From West Drayton they were continually being stopped by signals and they were informed that they would be turned into Hanwell Bridge siding, because of the congestion of the trains ahead. The driver brought the train to a stand clear of the main line at the stop signal close to Hanwell viaduct – itself a favourite target for Luftwaffe attacks. The signals and points controlling the outlet from these sidings were operated by a shunter signalman, but he was nowhere to be seen. The driver tried to contact control on the telephone, in order to establish if the train was to be left there, but could not get through. In the meantime, Summers walked back to the guard's van, only to discover that he also had gone.

Thus they were stranded, in the middle of the night, with an air raid raging all around them. They had been diverted off the main line to a siding to await orders, but now could not contact anyone and indeed no one else seemed particularly concerned about them. The Mogul, as the 2-6-0 class was also known, offered little in the way of overhead protection because the cab roof was shorter than that fitted on the 4-6-0 classes, making then feel increasingly vulnerable. The sound of exploding bombs was now very close, and they were a sitting target for any bomber, with nothing whatsoever with which to defend themselves. They could have abandoned the train, but Summers remembered later that this seemed like desertion, and in any case, there was nowhere that they could have gone that could have offered them any greater cover or protection. So they remained, listening to the bombs whistling down and the shrapnel rattling on the cab roof, watching the flames light up the sky and wondering if they would ever get home. It was a night that Summers would never forget. When he finally got home, he had been on duty for over twenty-four hours continuously. The ordeal was made all the worse for train crews working long distances, by the constant worry about what was happening at home and if their families were safe.

During the winter of 1940–1941 the daily news bulletins brought with them mounting horror as the stories of German air attacks intensified. At first, they were centred on London but as time went by, other cities were bombed. Coventry, Birmingham, Manchester, Bristol, Sheffield, each was attacked in turn. Coventry had been particularly shocking with reports filtering through of every railway line out of the city blocked for two days until gangs could clear some of them. Up to this point however, South Wales had been relatively fortunate. It was not until the bitterly cold New Year of 1941 that the region was hit hard. Hundreds of people were killed in Cardiff when that city was raided, the docks being the main target but Llandaff Cathedral was also badly damaged.

William John Whelan of Swansea was a docks traffic office telephonist, aged just 18 when his home town was attacked in January 1941. He was due to report to his switchboard down by the docks that night and had just entered the gates at 21.40 when a heavy high explosive bomb came down. The blast caught him sideways, but he went on his way in good order to the control office. On his arrival he was told in a casual way that incendiaries were dropping in numbers near the sheds. Finding no one handy to accompany him, Whelan went to K shed, where several incendiaries had come through the roof and had set fire to paper stored against the wall in one of the corners. Immediately he dealt with the unwelcome arrivals by carrying them outside, using a tinplate as a tray. Patiently he removed eight bombs, and then took four buckets into the shed to put out what was left of the fire. After satisfying himself that K shed was safe for the time being he went to H shed – directly opposite – where he found a soldier trying to cope with some bombs that had made a hole in the roof. He and the soldier extinguished the bombs, in spite of the fact that the raid was now at its peak and bombs were now falling from the sky in all directions.

Leaving H shed he made his way to the quayside where he put out more burning bombs. In doing so he noticed that part of L shed had caught fire, and so quickly fetched one of the AFS squads, showed them the quickest point at which they could bring their pumps into action, and lent a hand manning the hoses. As he was assisting the AFS he noticed that a run of railway wagons were lined up dangerously close to the burning shed. He called two of the AFS squad and a policeman to help him push the wagons out of harm's way. In manning the hoses however he had become soaked from head to toe in water, and so went back to the control office in the hope of finding a change of clothes. For the remainder of the raid he stayed at his post, carrying messages from the only remaining point connected by telephone to other points on the dock. Later, he would receive a personal letter conveying the congratulation of Minister of War Transport Lord Leathers on his award of the British Empire Medal (the first intimation he had received of the award). When he read it, he is reported to have commented that too much fuss was being made of the whole thing.

It was mid-February before the Blitz came in earnest to Swansea. Over 3 consecutive nights, more than 200 bombers flattened the entire centre of the town. Bill Morgan had been with GWR since 1916, but this would prove to be the most hazardous night of his career. It started with Morgan and fireman Ted Rees sitting in the back room of their lodgings in Landore, playing cards and listening to the wireless to pass the time. They were due at Landore station just after midnight where they would work their light Castle down to Swansea to couple up with the down parcels from Paddington. The sirens had first sounded in the late afternoon that day, and as the evening wore on, wave after wave of enemy aircraft had come over, some dropping flares as markers, later waves dropping incendiaries and heavy bombs.

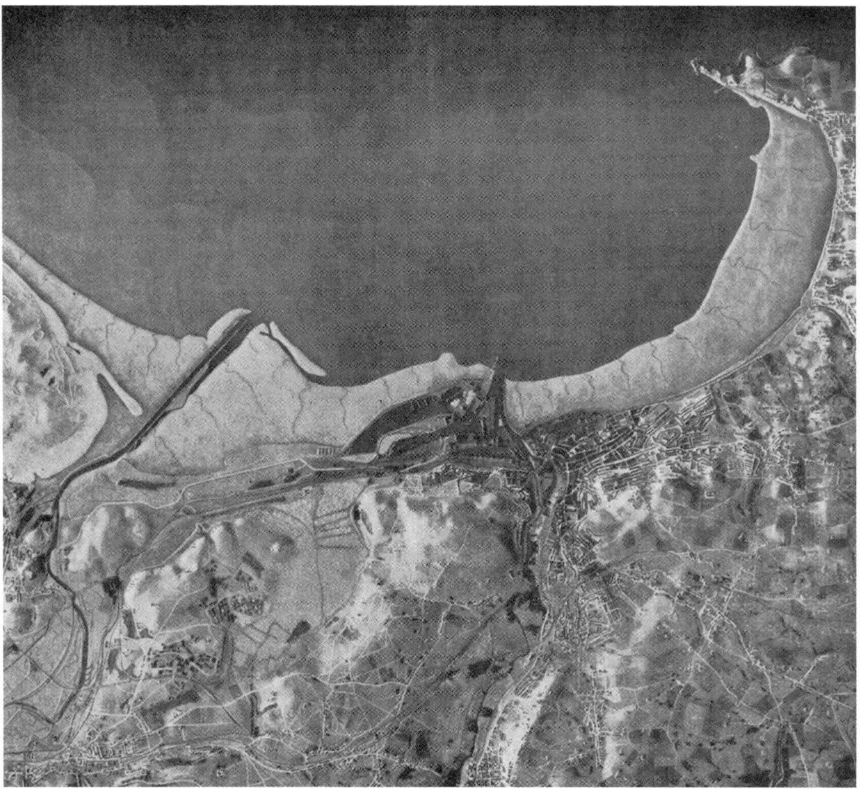

A Luftwaffe aerial photograph of Swansea, 1941. (Public Domain)

Landore and the surrounding towns were pounded mercilessly. Picking up their sandwiches and flasks of tea as they went, the two men headed out of their lodgings into the dark street. The air was rent by the thunderous din of guns and explosions, and the street was deserted apart from a lone ARP warden who, at first angry that civilians should be out of cover, shouted good luck to them once he realised that they were GWR men heading for the station. Both were now regretting the fact that they had no steel helmets. Each had been issued with one months before, and at first had carried them around religiously. However complacency had started to set in, and if a raid came whilst they were at home the helmet was likely to have been left at the shed. If it came whilst they were at the shed, the helmet was likely to be on the locomotive. Whenever they were needed they were not to hand, and Morgan's was at that particular moment hanging on the back of his pantry door at home. That belonging to Rees had not been seen since he left it on a loco several months before. Both were now regretting being so careless.

At the station, their Castle which they had left there earlier in the day was ready and prepared for them, and they took her out of Landore on time, in spite of the chaos all around. They worked light engine down to Swansea, and as they drew near to the town they kept a watchful eye on the track ahead in case of any obstruction. In the distance, the entire town seemed to be ablaze. There was no need to adjust the canvas cover on their cab as any glare from the firebox would be as nothing compared to the inferno raging all around them. Miraculously the line ahead was clear, but full of trepidation Rees and Morgan proceeded slowly, unsure of what to expect.

The signal was off for them to berth themselves in their siding whilst they waited for their counterpart Castle and crew to bring the parcels in from Paddington. They would pull into the buffers at Swansea and uncouple, whilst Bill and Ted coupled up to the rear and took the train on the remainder of its journey to Neyland. They were both anxious to be out of Swansea sidings where they were effectively sitting ducks as incendiaries fell all around them, doing little damage but starting small fires all over the tracks. They anticipated that with all the bombing and chaos around them, the down parcels train would be late, but as if by a miracle it steamed in exactly on time. It seemed unbelievable that points and communications should be working so efficiently in the midst of so much destruction.

Ted leapt up to the regulator in his eagerness to get under way. They watched the signal like a pair of hawks until it came off and as soon as it did so they were away. They steamed into the station, which was alive with scurrying figures, their faces a strange orange hue from the glare of the fires blazing all around. Bill jumped down from the footplate to the platform before the engine had actually come to a standstill, and could hardly get the coupling chains fastened quickly enough. He remembered:

> Suddenly it sounded as if all hell was let loose. The ground shook beneath us, the last remnants of the glass roof over the platform came crashing down about our heads and I flung myself down under the tender as twisted steel supports collapsed along the platform. Whistles were blowing, debris was flying, and in the uproar and confusion I suddenly noticed, with dismay, that every signal was on. Nobody and no loco was going anywhere. 'Take cover! Take cover!' the shouts rang out all over the station, as I heaved myself out from under the tender and climbed back on to the footplate to check with Ted. 'I wish I had my bloody helmet!' he shouted as I climbed back on to the footplate, and I mentally echoed his wish. The platforms were clearing rapidly as I dropped the dampers and closed the firebox door.
>
> 'Looks as if we're stuck here for the duration, so we'd better make ourselves comfortable,' I suggested, picking up my double-homer. 'Come on boy, under the tender with us.'
>
> 'Good idea, Bill,' he agreed, 'I don't fancy being too close to that scalding boiler, man, I can tell you.'
>
> We clambered down from the Castle and climbed down off the platform, settling ourselves by the middle wheel of the tender, our double-home boxes making convenient seats. We stayed there, wedged between tender and platform, for the next hour while the blitz continued relentlessly above and around us. At least we had the satisfaction of knowing that nothing short of a direct hit could affect us. We were supposed to be due out at 2.45, but it was not until nearly four o'clock that there was a slight lull in the bombing and we heard that wonderful sound of a guard's whistle! At least something was on the move at last, we thought, as we climbed out of our shelter and joined the other Company men, civilians, Civil Defence Workers, W.V.S. helpers and

> others who all suddenly appeared from heaven knows where.
>
> Within a few minutes we were given the signal, and getting steam up as fast as we could, we gratefully pulled out of Swansea Station, just as everyone was running for cover once more as another wave of bombers let loose their load of destruction on the town.[14]

It was as if they had just broken free of a blockade as they steamed through the blazing town. The tracks shone brightly as they reflected the light from the flashes of explosions and fires, and they cut a swathe through the rubble and scenes of destruction on either side of them. Several of the sidings had been hit, but the line they were on was remarkably straight and clear. They could hardly believe their good fortune as they rode through it all, as if the train that they were on was somehow charmed. They held their breath as they approached each signal in case it was against them, but each one turned out to be set in their favour and gradually they left the crippled town behind them. Still watching the track ahead for any sign of damage, after a dozen or so miles they approached their next stop, Llanelly.

They were now heading back into the inferno, as bells were ringing, whistles were blowing, there was shouting, confusion and chaos as they slowed down to a halt upon reaching the platform. The familiar low drone of enemy aircraft overhead could clearly be heard, and the few minutes that they had to wait stretched on for eternity. As they waited they paced around the cab in an attempt to ease the tension that they felt; they urgently wanted to get going once more. As soon as they had the road they steamed hurriedly away from the roar of collapsing buildings and the explosions of bombs. Once on the move, they were in their own world once more, and leaving behind the devastated industrial areas they approached the comparative calm of Carmarthen. Bill almost felt guilty at the feeling of safety which now came over him. The night was now peaceful, in contrast to the din of battle that they were leaving behind. On the horizon was visible an orange glow, which could be seen from Neyland, at least 80 miles away. They arrived at 8.45 that morning, and Morgan had never been more thankful to see the sight of the dirty old shed. He did not know it at the time but his brother-in-law was headed in the opposite direction with a train full of passengers bound for Swansea. He was destined to spend the night in a gutter, taking cover behind fallen masonry, as Swansea erupted all around him, though thankfully he survived.

Morgan and Rees headed back towards Llanelly and Swansea the following day. The scenes of destruction which met their gaze were difficult to comprehend. Landmarks had been destroyed, whole streets had disappeared under a mass of rubble, burnt out cars still smouldered, and those buildings which had been hit but were still standing stared rooflessly at the sky. They proceeded slowly as a speed restriction was in place, the tracks crowded with gangers, linesmen and engineers, repairing the damage as quickly as they could. Craters still gaped as they passed them, but the track had already been shored up by the labourers who toiled away to get things running again. Further away, civilians could be seen picking their way through the rubble. Some, men on their way to work, were carrying their bicycles over the cratered ground. Ashen faced women searched through the debris of what had once been their homes for any article which could be salvaged, whilst children, only aware of the novelty of the situation chattered excitedly, from the high vantage point of their cab, the two men had a grandstand view of this sad spectacle.

Two more Swansea employees of GWR, both shunters, also received the British Empire Medal for their courage during the Blitz, their names being Cyril Griffin (who had been awarded the Military Medal in the First World War) and Bryn Furneaux. Both men were working in an area which was showered with bombs during a night raid. The attack started at 19.52 and they were due to go off duty shortly, but worked on until 01.40 the following day.

An oblique Luftwaffe intelligence photograph of Swansea, the railway lines clearly visible. (Public Domain)

Incendiaries fell all around them, and when these were followed by high explosive bombs, all the shelter they could find was that offered by the foot of a wall against which they lay. They did not lie there for long however, as they moved about continually looking for fallen bombs. Some of the incendiaries which they tackled fell on railway wagons and on a shunter's cabin. Whilst they were dealing with this situation, some fire bombs fell in another yard, which they also tackled. Whilst doing this they went to the assistance of one of their colleagues, who had been rendered unconscious by a direct hit on the steel helmet by an incendiary. Having got him safely into shelter, they went to put out further fires in the fitting shops and around the electric cables. It was not until the time the raid ended that they dragged themselves wearily to bed.

Other acts of bravery in the South Wales Blitz went unrewarded. Frank Edward Martin, a 35-year old dock checker from Penarth near Cardiff who had joined the railway when he was 15, was at home drinking a cup of tea when he heard the 'alert' which was followed by the falling of incendiaries. Leaving home he ran down the hill to open the fire station. Carrying on, at the harbour office he met shunter Lewis who was a trained firefighter. He then asked for volunteers from a nearby air raid shelter to assist him. When no one would come forward, he and Lewis went on alone to No. 7 Fire Station and started up a mobile trailer pump. They loaded up the hand-gear and fire reel and took up position at the railway bridge nearby. A number of Nazi planes could be heard overhead, and a trail of incendiaries was falling across the harbour. Some of them had landed on top of some petrol storage tanks, presenting an imminent danger. Martin told Lewis to take the hoses down the road to the petrol tanks whilst he himself took a short-cut across the railway lines, carrying a fire shovel and a rake. When he reached the tanks, Martin, with the assistance of two Home Guards, smothered several incendiaries which had already been thrown down from the top of a tank by another helper.

Later, Martin and Lewis went along the railway lines, passing the harbour office, where they met a young lad named John Smith. The three together then put out incendiaries all along the line, and when near some sidings they saw other bombs burning amongst the wagons and also in a bomb crater. Martin dealt with the fire in the crater, whilst the others put out the fires spreading up the line. Ten minutes later, Martin was thrown to the ground by the blast from a bomb which exploded about 60 yards away. His legs were gashed and bleeding and his clothes torn to shreds. Picking himself up he discovered that Lewis and Smith had also been bowled over by the explosion. Undaunted, the three then proceeded to tackle a fire blazing in a yard some distance away. Upon getting closer they discovered that the source of the flames was a lorry piled high with timber. Both the cargo and the petrol tank were on fire but they managed to get the timber off the back, and used sheets of corrugated iron to contain the fire in the petrol tank.

The sky above had been quiet but now a growing hum signalled the return of the bombers, and explosives began to fall once more. Another large fire had broken out further up the road, and so the three men abandoned the hand gear and returned to the fire station to get the trailer pump. By this time they had acquired two more volunteers from a nearby air raid shelter as well as the assistance of shunter William Toye, an auxiliary fireman. He was not due to begin work until later that night, but chose to put his civic duty before his appointed clocking-in time. Together they pulled the heavy trailer pump, which weighed around a ton, until they came across an army lorry which towed the pump to the scene of the fire. Here, two small local authority pumps were on the point of running out of water so Martin arranged for the trailer pump to be connected to the nearest high pressure main and used it to relay water to the two smaller pumps. It was a grim task because in order to connect to the main, the bodies of several civilians killed by the bombs had to be moved to one side. The police were in due course informed of their location. It was by now around 22.30 and at this point three gasometers about 100 yards away received direct hits from bombs. The resulting explosion caused multiple injuries and Martin, Lewis, Smith and Toye attended to the wounded as best they could in the gas company's yard. At about 23.00 a hotel which had previously been hit caught fire in the basement, and as there were no firemen available to deal with it, Martin ordered the hose to be connected to the pump and the flames were thus brought under control. Bombs were still falling and several nearby houses were now on fire. Using rakes and shovels they cleared bombs from the road and tackled the burning upper floors of the houses with stirrup pumps until firemen arrived. As an indication of how bitterly cold this night was, water that they had drawn into buckets for the stirrup pumps was now beginning to freeze. The official report of this incident states that: 'Martin proceeded to the Police Station and asked the GWR Docks Control for relief men to be sent.

This could not be arranged for some time, and Martin therefore continued to fight fires until 6.00am.'[15]

Whilst Martin received the British Empire Medal, no official recognition was given to Lewis, Smith or Toye for their heroic actions that night.

In spite of the hardships of the war (or perhaps because of them) railway social events still continued. There were GWR ambulance dances, the church socials, the whist drives and the numerous chapel eisteddfods. Great care had to be taken when arranging choir anthems, however, or it might become apparent when it was too late that both bass performers were on a locomotive half way to Carmarthen! Bill Morgan had sometimes had to perform the tenor part alone, when GWR duty had claimed the rest of the St Clement's tenors. With so many men away at the front, the voices of the male railwaymen were in great demand during the war.

Even when not directly under attack, wartime conditions made life on the railway hard. Morgan remembered one pitch black night that winter of 1940–1941, at the Neyland shed. In the sky above could be heard the steady drone of high-flying bombers on their way to attack Liverpool. As a result, the station was on alert blackout and practically everything came to a standstill, as everyone sat in the dark and waited. All lights were extinguished, and all fireboxes closed down. Shunting was stopped, and an eerie silence descended on the yard, broken only by the seemingly endless droning of the bombers overhead. They took so long to pass that several hundred must have been involved. Morgan was sitting on the footplate of a small tank engine with Tom the chargeman, smoking a cigarette in a cupped hand to avoid showing any light. Suddenly the pair became aware of the sound of splashing water coming from the other side of the yard. Both men peered hard into the darkness but could see nothing. Eventually Tom broke the stillness of the night by calling out, 'Anybody there?'

'I can't shut the valve off!' came a desperate cry from the darkness. It appeared that one of the young cleaners was in trouble, and Tom decided to go and help him. The valve controlled the supply of water to the engines, and one appeared to have just filled up with water when the cleaner realised that he couldn't turn it off, resulting in water flooding the yard. In the pitch blackness nothing could be seen, however, and so the chargeman asked Bill for a flare lamp to light his way. Still conscious of the drone from above, he opened the firebox just a fraction, lit a small flare lamp and tried his best to shield it with his hand. As he passed it over he reminded his colleague to do likewise, less they be seen from the sky. Tom heeded the warning and had only gone a few yards when he disappeared into the darkness. Still puffing on his cigarette, Bill peered into the blackness, wondering what had happened. The chargeman should have reached the other side of the yard by now but water was still audibly running. He was all set to venture out and find out himself what was going on, when there was an almighty roar, and the most extraordinary sight met his eyes. An enormous flame leapt some 30 feet into the air, illuminating the entire scene as the cleaner ran for his life down the line and Tom stared in disbelief at the flaming torch now towering above him.

In an instant Morgan understood what must have happened. The gas valve and water valve were next to each other, and somehow in the darkness the wrong valve had been turned. The flare lamp had ignited the escaping gas like a blow torch! He grabbed two shovels from the cab and raced to the scene, where Tom was trying desperately to throw handfuls of dirt and ash to stop the jet of flame, as it was impossible to get near enough to turn it off. With a shovel each, the two started heaping earth up on to it as the yard suddenly sprang to life with men appearing out of the previously darkened corners, shouting (as if any encouragement were needed) 'Put that light out!' What the hell do they think we are doing, Morgan thought, as he shovelled away desperately, the drone of engines still menacingly loud overhead. Men came running with more shovels, the yard now lit up like daylight. Eventually the giant Roman candle was brought under control, the water was turned off and the yard was darkened once more. The tension was palpable however as they waited for the crash of bombs from above, but nothing came. The drone of engines continued unchanged; if the Luftwaffe did notice, they chose not to deviate from their assigned target.

Early in the war GWR had begun to recruit women to replace men as more and more staff were called up to join the armed forces, leading to sometimes amusing situations. Firemen like Morgan had gradually become used to the sight of women working on the platforms, always dressed smartly in jackets and skirts. One morning around this time however he was surprised to see, as he looked over the side of his cab, the lone figure of what he took to be a man on the track, waving his hands backward and forward above his head. With much cursing about what kind of bloody fool would do such a thing, Ted the driver pulled off the regulator and slammed on the brakes. As the locomotive slowed to a halt however their assumptions were proved to be wrong, as they drew alongside the figure proved to be a woman. She was wearing company uniform including – much to their astonishment – trousers. This was something that they had never encountered before. To add to the incongruous nature of the sight before them, the woman's uniform was at least two sizes too big for her, and the trousers, which were made of stiff heavy serge, made her legs look like two black telegraph poles under her jacket.

Sheepishly the woman asked if she could have a lift, explaining that it was her job to light the signal lamps – she carried a can of paraffin as proof – and that because they were so far apart it would take her all day if she had to walk. Now it became apparent why she had been given a uniform including trousers – it would not have been considered seemly for her to climb to the top of a ladder wearing a skirt. They hauled her up on to the footplate and she perched on the fireman's tip seat clutching her paraffin can as they proceeded along the line. Morgan was curious as to why she was not carrying lit replacement lamps with her, as per normal practice. She conceded that this was what she was supposed to do, but as the filled lamps were too heavy for her, she found it easier to top up and light the ones that were already in situ. They dropped her at the next signal, with a warning not to flag down an engine from the centre of the track next time. Later that day, returning along the same stretch of line they encountered her sitting forlornly at the bottom of one of the signals, almost lost in her oversized uniform. Slowing down, they asked her what the matter was. Looking up sadly, she informed them that she had forgotten the matches.

The number of women employed by the Great Western before the war was 1,623. With the coming of war that number rapidly increased by 10,671 to 12,294. By the war's end the number of women of all grades in the service of GWR would reach 18,542. Besides those in roles as train announcers, ticket collectors, van girls, office messengers, lift attendants, train indicator board operators, and level crossing keepers, some forty-eight were employed in the company's police department. The most skilled job on any railway was undoubtedly that of signalman. The locomotive drivers were sincere in their respect of these men who were their guardians (no driver would ever refer to one as a signalman however, they were always 'bobbies', in reference to the fact that in the earliest rulebooks reference was always made to them as 'policemen'). Yet more and more women were now being trained to do duty in the signal box. Journalist Collie Knox commented:

> There was an era, I must freely confess, when I myself would have raised an eyebrow or two at the arrival of signal-women. But that would have been in peace-time. This war has taught me, as it has taught millions of other men, that women are creatures of extraordinary adaptability. They are doing men's jobs not only enthusiastically but astonishingly well, and in any mechanical work they are showing a proficiency which would make, and most understandably, their grandmothers turn somersaults in their graves.[16]

The only thing that puzzled him about signalwomen was where they would find the physical strength to work the heavy levers. By the middle of the war, the National Union of Railwaymen would pass a resolution at its conference calling for equal pay for all rail-women, a testament to the level of respect that they had earned.

One particular woman with enormous mental strength, not to mention presence of mind was Mrs Florence Ross, a postal sorter at Paddington station during an intense attack in April 1941. The station had narrowly avoided disaster the previous month when direct hits were made on Paddington by high explosives and incendiaries. One bomb exploded on platforms 6 and 7, making a 40-foot-wide crater, some 12 feet deep. On that occasion by the same evening all obstructed lines were restored except No. 6 and 7, which were reopened later in the week. Now, when the first bombers came over again, Mrs Ross sought safety in a shelter underneath platform 1. A minute

Newly recruited Signal Women receive instructions in how to operate a Signal Box.

afterwards the platform was bombed. All the shelter lights went out, and the rescuers worked by the glow of torches and hurricane lamps. This was where Mrs Ross stepped in. She called for bandages and a first aid kit. All through that dreadful night she tended and comforted the injured passengers and the stationmaster told her that it was one of the finest acts he had ever seen. He subsequently presented her, on behalf of the staff of platform 1, with an inscribed cigarette case. Prior to becoming a sorter she had been a trained nurse and ran a health clinic at Golders Green. Her bravery that night was also recognised by the award of the George Medal.

On 20 March 1941, the air raid sirens were heard at Plymouth. GWR district horse inspector William Sparks had his home above the stables. When the sirens went off that evening his wife and daughter went into the shelter Sparks and his son Frank (who was also a railway employee) went to check on the horses. Almost immediately Frank was knocked out by an incendiary. His father dragged him out as a bomb fell on the stables. Meanwhile the oil storage shed had caught fire. Frank had recovered somewhat and was now able to help his father empty buckets of water onto the flames. The terrified horses were kicking madly but father and son managed to get them all away safely. This was not the only incident in which great bravery was shown in the rescue of animals. James George Thomas, stableman and Thomas Penwill, temporary carter, of Great Western Railway were both awarded the British Empire Medal for their bravery at this time. During the intense air raid on Plymouth Thomas and Penwill were also on duty at railway stables when adjoining premises were set on fire. The two men began transfer the fifty horses to a safer place when two high explosive bombs fell on the stables and both men were injured. After they had received first aid the two men continued working, and twenty-two of the horses were saved. The conditions in which this work was carried out were extremely dangerous, and Penwill and Thomas showed considerable courage and determination.

The fact that the railway establishment at this time was still a network of private companies was at times a major contributing factor to the morale and fortitude of the employees. There was a strong sense of paternalism within them, and a railway company was often compared to a family. This engendered a certain sense of pride and loyalty among employees which might have been lacking had they been servants of a faceless state operated network. At Keyham, the station which served Devonport dockyard, there were several nights of heavy raids in April 1941. In one of these, Frederick John Harris, a grade 1 parcels porter, beset on all sides by flames and expecting to be knocked off his feet by an explosion at any time, stopped in his task of trying to find incendiaries among wagons full of munitions when he became aware that one of the fire bombs had fallen among a wagon of live pigs, which were now squealing shrilly. With stoical regard for the reputation of his employers for the safe carriage of goods, alive or dead, Harris refused to open the carriage and release the pigs which would then scatter in all directions; instead, he extinguished the bomb amongst them before returning to his other duties. The official citation for his award of the British Empire Medal read:

> Harris was in charge of a railway station on three consecutive nights during air raids – wagons and goods sheds contained high-explosives and oil – his action saved the goods shed and station buildings, private property and the lives of civilians in the street alongside – his example was an inspiration.[17]

Afterwards he was interviewed about the incident by a newspaper reporter, and commented:

> It is my wife who stuck at home through the blitzes and looked after me, who deserves a medal. I couldn't have kept going without her. It was very nasty while it lasted those three nights. Worse than anything I went through in France

> last time. The third night was the worst. I was all alone with the bombs and the oil and explosives. I had to hop from drum to drum putting out the fire bombs and one just missed my tin hat.[18]

An extremely modest man, in addition to his heroism at Keyham, on the night of 21 April, Harris was also engaged in extinguishing fires at nearby Ford Halt, working on a wooden platform which threatened to collapse at any moment, until the water supply ran out. Whilst he was engaged in this work, delayed-action bombs were dropped within a few yards of the platform constituting a grave danger. He continued, however, to combat the fire until lack of water made it impossible to persist. There was no doubt that his example and leadership were an inspiration to the other men involved, and resulted in saving much property and probably also several lives. Frederick John Harris, of Gordon Terrace, Mutley, Plymouth had been employed by GWR for twenty-two years in 1941. For his efforts he was originally recommended for a George Medal, but this was amended and he instead received the British Empire Medal.

In May 1941, during the Merseyside Blitz, Horace Wigfield, a supernumerary goods porter received a 'commendation' for his unselfish service during an air raid. The Birkenhead area in which he worked was receiving a heavy bombardment when a call went out for volunteers to assist in removing two men who had been injured by bombs at the cattle-landing stage next to the goods station. Wigfield offered his services and, carrying a stretcher, went with two other men to the danger spot. They found on arrival that the floating-bridge leading from the highway over the river to the landing-stage had collapsed in two places. At one point it was necessary, in order to get across, to walk for a distance of 4 feet along a beam 8 inches in width, over a yawning hole. This would have been enough to strain the nerve of even Houdini, for one false step would have plunged the victim into the river. At the second point of damage the skip break in the bridge structure had to be skirted, and the whole proceeding was extremely dangerous. The night was as dark as pitch and the only light available came from an electric torch. Even this had to be used sparingly for fear of alerting marauding bombers above. Yet Wigfield and a companion named Jackson managed to carry one of the seriously injured men on a stretcher from the landing stage to the ambulance. Then they went back for the other casualty. The nerve of both men in going back a second time across the damaged floating roadway, knowing the dangers, was worthy of note.

Another Birkenhead resident and GWR employee was shunter Norman Tunna, who was the first railway worker and the first Merseyside man to be awarded the George Cross, the highest civilian award for bravery. In many ways the shunters were the unsung heroes of the railway network during this part of the war. Small cogs in a mighty machine, the shunters carried on their unglamorous jobs with a sublime indifference to the crashing of bombs or to the devastation of fire. How they managed to shunt train after train in the blackout escaped the comprehension of many, but somehow they managed it. When air raid warnings were expected early in the evening the shunters concentrated all their energy on shunting traffic for departing trains before the sirens started their chilling whine. Although they were allowed to use a white

Shunter Norman Tunna of Birkenhead was awarded the George Cross for bravery during an air raid in 1940. (Public Domain)

light for shunting during air raids, many tried, in the interests of the marshalling yards themselves and the houses which surrounded them, to keep this to a minimum. One of the shunters was quoted as saying:

> We carry on in this way up to the time the guns in the immediate vicinity start their music – and what a noise it is! The high pitch of the mobile, the bang of the 'Chicago pianos' and the deep boom of the bigger guns make a din that will not easily be forgotten by those who have experienced it during the constant raids and bombing we have had in the London area since the intensified night attacks began.[19]

Tunna was at his shunting work during a raid on the Port of Liverpool when the German raid began. *The London Gazette* provided details of the events which resulted in his award, and recorded that:

> A large number of incendiary bombs fell on and about the goods station and sidings. Amongst the wagons in the yards were a train load of ammunition, various trucks of petrol in tins, bombs and ammunition fuses. Most of the enemy incendiary bombs were extinguished by the prompt action of the staff on duty before damage could be done, but a serious fire developed from incendiaries falling in one section of the station premises. In the course of these events Shunter Tunna discovered two incendiary bombs burning in a sheeted open wagon, containing 250lb bombs. With complete disregard for personal risk, Tunna removed the sheet, extinguished the incendiary bombs and removed them from the truck. The top layer of these heavy bombs was hot. Tunna's action displayed courage in a very high degree and eliminated the risk of serious explosions, the result of which it would be difficult to measure.[20]

As he worked to remove them, molten metal from one of the incendiaries, which was actually jammed between the bombs, was steadily dripping down. Tunna continues the story in his own words:

> An ammunition train loaded with high-explosive bombs had been taken out of the yard and was awaiting the signals when the raiders began to drop incendiary bombs. I had been the shunter on the train. As I was walking down the side of it I saw that incendiary bombs had dropped into one wagon and that the sheet-covering was ablaze. I went to the engine, got a bucket of water and threw it onto the wagon. The sheet continued to burn fiercely, so I went round the wagon, undid the ropes and tore off the burning sheet. I then got the stirrup-pump and a bucket of water. I got into the wagon and found that a burning incendiary was jammed between two of the H.E. bombs.
>
> I could not move the incendiary with my hands, so I got my shunter's pole and forced the two big bombs apart. I was then able to throw out the incendiary. The top layer of bombs was very hot, so I sprayed them with water from the stirrup-pump. I should like to pay tribute to the help I had from Fireman Frank Newns, who carried buckets of water to me, and also to Driver Ivor Davies, who got into the wagon and helped me with the pump.[21]

Of Tunna's comrades that night, cartage foreman William Edwin Weaver received the British Empire Medal, foreman Thomas also was awarded the British Empire Medal, whist driver Davies, fireman Newns and goods checker Patrick Mahoney were all decorated with the George Medal, the latter for leading his gang in subduing the flames and moving cases of ammunition fuses away from centres of fire.

Davies and Newns were both members of the Associated Society of Locomotive Engineers and Firemen. In paying

The George Cross, Britain's highest award for bravery not in the face of the enemy. (Public Domain)

tribute to them in its official history published just after the war, the union noted dryly that these were but two instances of sheer courage shown by the members of the society in the nation's darkest hour. And yet the general secretary had to negotiate for six months before railwaymen were given a wage increase, and even then this was not adequate to meet the higher cost of living resulting from the war. At the union's 1941 conference, the 4s per week pay award was criticised as meagre. The same conference drew attention to the irregular nature of the shifts of footplate crew, and the long hours they were often expected to work. The gruelling nature of these shifts were exacerbated by the lack of any provision for food, and delegates called for canteens to be set up, as had been done in other industries where workers were expected to put in long hours as part of the war effort.

A typical example of this lack of provision comes from Jack Gardner, who was a GWR fireman working from Didcot into London during the Blitz. As far as bombing was concerned he was lucky, his 08.10 departure often taking him out of the capital just as the raids were beginning in earnest, and at worst he was troubled by the patter of shrapnel from British anti-aircraft guns booming on Wormwood Scrubs as he passed by. He remembered that instead:

> Overtime and the privations that accompanied it were the worst of our troubles. There was a long period

> when overtime took us right round the clock, having taken only enough food for a normal day. This could not be attributed to bad planning, rations didn't allow more. I was hungry many times before the situation improved with the provision of canteens at some of some of the main line stations. At least it eased the pangs of hunger some of the time. Being cold, wet and hungry in the frost of winter and shivering even with an overcoat on with a fire in the box seemed unlikely but it was true. When standing in a loop waiting our turn to go it was necessary to keep the fire low to avoid blowing off steam to conserve water – cold comfort with a low fire. I can recall one particular night when I was stopped at the 'Intermediate Block signal' between Wantage and Challow. There was just a signal and telephone, no actual signal box for warmth. We were enveloped in a blanket of freezing fog and a foot of snow lay on the ground. The east wind blew in from the back, the little heat which came from the fire-hole doors was lost. The continuous trek to the phone had cut a rut in the snow, the only sign of any movement.[22]

Despite these early hardships, the railwaymen recognised that they were an essential part of the war effort. Great Western Railway, perhaps more than any of the 'Big Four', was a railway of personality. It was the only one to have retained its identity through the Grouping Act. Its service during the war was of colossal magnitude, and whilst a railway is comprised of mechanical components and machinery, it is the men and women who operate that machinery who make it what it is. Human endeavour is paramount, and in the service of their country at this most pressing of times, the personnel of GWR neither stumbled nor faltered.

Chapter Four

SOUTHERN RAILWAY IN THE FIRING LINE

Southern Railway (SR), sometimes shortened just to 'Southern', was established in the 1921 Grouping Act. It linked London with the Channel ports, South West England, south coast resorts and Kent. The railway was formed by the amalgamation of several smaller railway companies, the largest of which were London and South Western Railway (LSWR), London, Brighton and South Coast Railway (LB & SCR) and South Eastern and Chatham Railway (SE & CR). The construction of what was to become Southern Railway began in 1838 with the opening of the London and Southampton Railway, which was later renamed London and South Western Railway. The railway was noted for its astute use of public relations and a coherent management structure headed by Sir Herbert Walker. At 2,186 miles (3,518km), Southern Railway was the smallest of the 'Big Four' railway companies and, unlike the others, the majority of its revenue came from passenger traffic rather than freight. By the outbreak of the Second World War, it had also created what was at that time the world's largest electrified railway system, with most of the lines immediately south of London converted to this method of power.

During the early part of the war, Southern Railway workshops (like those of other companies) were underutilised, and despite their obvious suitability for heavy engineering work, and the efforts of the various chief mechanical engineers to obtain contracts for war materials, they were dealing with only a fraction of the workload for which they had capacity. The policy of the Ministry of Labour in response to this situation was not one of attempting to direct more essential war work to them, but instead they chose to direct spare or unemployed labour out of the workshops and into other industries. These resulted in such anomalies as a foreman from a railway works being deployed in the somewhat alien environment of an aircraft factory. In the autumn of 1940, Mr A.L. Mieville – a senior technical officer from the Ministry of Labour headquarters in London – undertook a whirlwind tour of thirteen railway workshops in the course of a week or so, in the quest for evidence of the need for such workshops to divest themselves of surplus labour. He recorded of his visit to the Eastleigh works:

> The SR gave me the impression that they won't play ball. All the Chiefs seemed to feel hurt. I repeatedly had to ask them to forget about the past. They seem to be sore all over and some of the officials were hardly polite until the ice had been thawed. Their obvious resentment against the Ministry of Labour should not have been allowed to arise.[1]

In case it should be thought that it was Southern Railway alone where there was resentment, Mieville also recorded that the atmosphere was frigid and unfriendly at most of the LNER workshops that he visited. None the less, he seems to have undergone some form of Damascene conversion during his tour, as his report concluded that the best use of the skills present in the railway workshops was to direct more work to them, rather than to denude them of labour. Never the less the impression seems to have persisted at the Ministry of Labour that Southern Railway was not pulling its weight in terms of war production. A few months later the engineering director had to assure the ministry that government work always took priority over its own construction programme, and that an offer made to the Ministry of Supply to set up a shell production shop at Eastleigh had come to nothing.

As well as recruiting more women into formerly male roles, railways attempted to alleviate wartime staff shortages by recalling retired members of staff. Mr S.C. Lang, who had formerly held the position of stationmaster at Vauxhall and Queens Road, had returned from retirement to assist the company during the national emergency. He was knocked down and killed instantly by an electric train on 5 June 1940. Before his retirement Mr Lang was awarded the Gold Medal for fifty years continuous service. It was a testament to his character that Lang found it impossible to remain at home whilst the company had need of his services. Lang had actually retired a considerable length of time before the war – on 1 November 1932, at age 61. He was therefore in his late sixties when he resumed his post as stationmaster at Vauxhall, which included supervision of Queens Road and the locomotive junction signal box between the two stations. After what was described as a 'routine visit' to the box, Lang climbed down the staircase at the south end, reaching ground level at 'a wide space between the down local and a coal siding.' He started to cross the running lines, pausing for an unknown reason between the rails of the down through line. The driver of an electric train on the up local line noticed this, and sounded his whistle. Lang did not respond 'until the train was within a short distance of him. He then suddenly stepped forward onto the up local line', where he was hit and killed 'in spite of the motorman's efforts to avoid the accident.'

An inspector observed in his report that between Lang's retirement and his return to work, the lines had been rearranged, including reversing the direction trains were travelling in on the two lines concerned. Lang knew about this, so the inspector could only speculate that he became confused and instinctively started to move from one line to the next, believing himself to be stepping into a safer position. Why Lang was on the tracks at all was unclear: 'His motive for retracing his steps southwards instead of continuing northwards is obscure – as also his reason for being on the tracks.' He was expected to be returning to either Queens Road or Vauxhall station 'and as there was a safe route available to either place clear of all running lines he was remiss in attempting to go via the track.' The inspector's conclusion was therefore that Lang 'took a wholly unnecessary risk and must be held responsible for the accident.'[2]

During the early years of the war, J.N. Faulkner commuted daily from Surbiton to the city and kept meticulous records describing how the South Western section of Southern Railway carried on operating during the Blitz. Note-taking on stations or in trains was regarded as a highly suspicious activity during the tense months of 1940, so all observations had to be memorised until they could be committed to paper at home that evening. Immediately after the fall of France the Luftwaffe began reconnaissance in force over southern England. On 20 June 1940, one of these found the Southern Railway's Redbridge permanent way depot, and 7,000 sleepers along with 2,000 crossing timbers were set on fire. Enemy air activity at first concentrated on ports and harbours, with Portsmouth being attacked at midday on 12 August. At the harbour station the landing stage was badly damaged by a bomb and the platforms set on fire, and several locomotives were also destroyed. Services continued from the two remaining platforms, with the station back in full use by the end of October.

The next day, Southampton docks was the target in the first of a series of raids. On 14 August, the 15.05 service from Bournemouth West to Waterloo was derailed by a bomb which landed directly in front of the train, the loco (No. 860 *Lord Hawke*) and the leading van both falling into the crater, fortunately without serious casualties. The incident was attended by a rerailing gang, known as the 'heavy lifters' including Bill Bishop. He remembered that they and their crane left the depot with all speed to attend the scene, even though the raid was still on:

> The down line had also been damaged in the attack so we could not even get close to help, having to retire

> to Swaythling Goods Yard, the nearest place available until the platelayers repaired the line. It was night time before we could return to the scene and it was with some trepidation that we started our work. In the sky, not far away, was a huge glow caused by a massive fire burning in the Docks, as a result of a raid on a butter store the night before. I decided that if we came under attack again, I would take cover in a nearby ditch, we were though left in peace that night, the raiders not returning. The weight of the engine was too much for our crane alone, so we sought the assistance of Fratton, both cranes managing the operation together. Because of the angle of the engine we had to run alongside and lift one end at a time, slewing it over and then manoeuvring the cranes a little nearer. Eventually it was accomplished, the tender being easily placed behind the engine, having lost most of its load of coal in the process. The bomb crater was then filled in and the track repaired in the space of a few hours, a remarkable achievement by those concerned.[3]

Both lines were functioning again by midday on 15 August, though no details of this incident were published at the time due to wartime censorship. From then on, most rerailing work was carried out in daylight as the lights necessary to work at night were too much of a target for the enemy. Even though there was a war on, this kind of work was entirely voluntary as it was so risky. At this early stage, the efforts of the Luftwaffe were not primarily directed against railways. Airfields and aircraft factories were their main targets and any damage to railway property or equipment tended to be incidental, though this did not mean that it was not highly destructive when it did occur. On 16 August one bomb, and machine gun fire damaged the 16.49 service from Waterloo to Kingston roundabout at Malden, killing one of the passengers. A second bomb dropped at the same time struck the upside booking office with nine people killed in the booking hall and on the stairs to the local platform. Another

Southern Railway loco No 860 *Lord Hawke*, seen before the war. (Author's Collection)

bomb demolished West Barnes Crossing box on the Epsom line and a fourth left a 10-foot-deep crater across the junction at Merton Park on the Wimbledon to West Croydon line. Track damage was not serious, and Malden platform would reopen the following morning.

Around the same time a bomb had fallen near milepost 44 between Hook and Basingstoke, blocking the down lines. The debris was cleared and normal working resumed at 05.30 on 17 August, until further examination of the site at midday revealed an unexploded bomb. All traffic was then stopped. The army quickly arrived to deal with it, but unfortunately it exploded the following morning, killing four soldiers who were working on it. The delayed-action bomb, or more often the unexploded (dud) bomb or anti-aircraft shell was to become a major source of dislocation on the railways as the Blitz intensified. Many reported unexploded bombs proved upon investigation to be false alarms, often after traffic had been stopped for several hours. Genuine devices required the attention of the army's overstretched bomb disposal squads, though the landmines which were also dropped were the responsibility of the Royal Navy. Eventually volunteer railwaymen were trained to confirm the evidence of unexploded bombs and to carry out the preliminary stages of making them safe for traffic to pass.

Rules governed whether or not freight traffic might pass the scene, according to the size and proximity of the suspected bomb. Passenger traffic might also be allowed through if a screen of loaded coal wagons could be positioned to provide a blast shield. The Regional Civil Defence authorities had three categories of urgency to which they could allocate each incident – (a) being the most urgent, on lines vital to the war effort, (b) indicating less urgent but still to be tackled within ninety-six hours and (c) secondary lines to be cleared when possible. A bomb which fell on the picturesque Bluebell line in September 1940 fell into this last category and was left for ten days before removal. Southern Railway sometimes expressed exasperation with the category to which an incident was allocated, notably on one occasion when Clapham Junction was brought to a complete standstill.

Raids continued day and night, but up to this point little damage had been done in the inner London area. However, following the successful daylight raid on the docklands of 7 September 1940, a night raid brought the first of ninety-two bombs which would hit the lines into Waterloo. At 23.20 a bomb struck arch 161 of the viaduct at Juxton Street, Lambeth, between Vauxhall and Waterloo. The piers under two tracks on the Windsor line side were toppled off their foundations, the arches carrying the next four tracks fell, leaving the rails suspended over a 50-foot gap, and only the two main local lines remained standing somewhat precariously. In response, the remaining arches were shored up and a limited goods service was resumed on these two lines, subject to speed and weight restrictions. Clapham Junction continued to function, despite a bomb falling on the carriage sheds which wrecked a number of vehicles and blocked six sidings.

On Sunday morning, 8 September, Clapham Junction was operating a reduced service but at dusk the sirens sounded again warning of another night attack. Around 23.00 a bomb fell on the terminal platforms at Wimbledon, at the same time as a district line train was arriving, injuring nine passengers and staff, whilst another device fell nearby at Wimbledon Park sidings, damaging an empty train. With traction current lost, all movement through Wimbledon ceased. At Surbiton the following morning platforms were still occupied by trains which had been prevented from running the previous day, and no up trains would be leaving the station that morning. A damaged bridge between Putney and Wandsworth further added to the disruption. Buses were being used in part to get commuters into London, no trains running at all at this point on the district line. Communications were restored with Broad Street station later that morning, when damaged tracks were re-laid around the edge of an enormous bomb crater. This situation highlighted the fact that if business activity was to continue in the City of London, in spite of the heavy bombing, then information on alternative means of transport had to be made readily available to commuters. Using the press or radio would have given away information unnecessarily to the enemy, so Southern Railway opened up enquiry booths at many of its suburban stations while in Central London information kiosks were situated in the streets, usually near Underground stations, which exhibited blackboards showing the situation on each route and with a member of staff on duty to answer questions. As an aside, travelling on the Underground system at this time could be equally unnerving, as one newspaper correspondent observed:

> Not being one of those people who get a thrill from air raids (they are a rapidly diminishing number, by the way) nor possessing either a greater degree of courage or indifference than the next man in facing them, I have never felt so lonely

> as when travelling home at night on the District Railway when the blitz is on. Usually, one is the sole occupant of a long carriage in total darkness. The train crawls, partly to give the driver plenty of time to pull up if the track is broken, and partly in order to avoid hitting the points at such a pace as will cause vivid electric sparks to betray the presence of the line. Through the windows one watches the gun flashes and the shell bursts, and at the stations the drone of enemy planes can be heard. It is altogether an eerie feeling of helplessness, and I am always glad to face the ten minutes' walk home from the station through the deserted streets. There at least, one can dive for cover if anything is heard falling. Last night the tension of what to me is always a bit of an ordeal was broken by an amusing incident. The train had pulled up at a station. The automatic doors were opened, letting in a draught of icy air. Eight guns went off more or less simultaneously in a predicted concentration, but before the shells began to go 'Pop pop pop' some two miles up in the sky there was a yell from a fellow passenger in the next carriage, 'Hi porter, guard,' he cried, and the natural thought was that he had been hit by something. But no. This was his complaint as I overheard it: 'These doors began to open, I started to walk out and they closed again. Now they have caught my head and I can't move.' So while the guns continued to fire the guard had to tackle the door release mechanism to release the man who was thus imprisoned. His was a predicament most Underground passengers have imagined but few have seen.[4]

One man who showed great bravery, during a raid on a Southern Railway yard at Hither Green in London, was yardmaster Harold John Savage. In September 1940, one of ten waggons containing explosives was set alight by incendiaries. Savage managed to uncouple the blazing truck. The floorboards were burning but, crawling under the waggon, Savage played a hose on the

The George Medal, frequently awarded for acts of heroism in the Blitz of 1940-41. (Public Domain)

flames until they were extinguished and the threat of a disastrous explosion was averted. Savage had been with the railway since he was 14 years old, following in the footsteps of his father and great uncle. For this incident he received the George Medal.

On 10 September, Waterloo station was closed to ordinary traffic, but trains were running once more to Clapham Junction, which handled most of the traffic usually bound for Waterloo whilst it was out of service. For the next three days much changing of engines took place at Surbiton because M7 tank engines were the heaviest locomotives allowed over the fragile arches at Juxon Street. Interruptions to the loading of mails and papers at Waterloo as a result of imminent danger warnings became much worse, and two days later the 22.30 Dorchester mail train did not reach Surbiton until 07.30 the next morning. The journey for commuters into London that morning was slow, but when the train eventually pulled into Holborn Viaduct they met Winston Churchill and his entourage on their way to inspect anti-invasion defences in East Kent, where a German landing was expected any day. Holborn Viaduct was the only Southern Railway terminus open that morning.

The situation changed again on the night of 12–13 September, when a bomb damaged Clapham Junction 'A' signal box before its protective canopy could be completed, as well as the Windsor line tracks, whilst an unexploded bomb was thought to be lying on platform 5 between the down main through and up main local lines. All traffic was halted on both the western and central sections until the bomb, which turned out to have a delayed-action fuse, exploded on the morning of 14 September. Another delayed-action device was revealed by clearance work on the same platform. The army was unable to dispose of this, and when it too went off the following day it demolished buildings and awnings on platform 5 (many of which were never replaced) and blocked all the south western main lines.

The situation at Clapham Junction (Britain's busiest interchange) was further complicated by another bomb lying at the country end of the Windsor line platforms which closed this part of the station until the afternoon of 16 September, with full restoration of service taking several more weeks. The Windsor lines were also hit by a bomb at bridges 11 and 12, close to West London Junction signal box. This also blocked the Longhedge lines underneath, until single line working was introduced again on 16 September. Nearby, a delayed-action bomb in a dangerous condition was found at Pouparts Junction, which affected both central and western sections. Even after the central side of Clapham Junction had been reopened, this device still prevented trains from reaching Victoria.

Southern Railway services terminated at either Putney or Earlsfield while removal of debris continued on the South Western platforms, but even when the station had been cleared, local line trains could not use Clapham Junction because they had to run to West London Junction in order to reverse, and this crossover was within the danger area of the Pouparts Junction bomb. The army eventually succeeded in sandbagging this sufficiently so that on 18 September engines could once again reach Nine Elms loco depot via the sidings at West London Junction, and from the following day trains could again pass on the south western lines, after the bomb was finally dealt with in a controlled explosion that afternoon.

Whilst Clapham Junction had been out of action, electric trains had been terminating at Wimbledon or Earlsfield, using the emergency crossovers there, and steam trains ran to and from Woking, only the mail and newspaper trains coming any closer to Waterloo. Wimbledon West yard was kept busy at this time, with no fewer than six 4-6-0s present on 16 September and another in the station on the up Dorchester mail. Once the blockage at Clapham Junction had been cleared, inner suburban electrics and a few main line steam trains resumed running to Waterloo from midday on 19 September, using the two local lines with a 10mph speed restriction at Juxton Street. On 25 September, the through lines were reopened and near normal services on the main line side were restored. From 1 October, Windsor line services resumed, using two tracks which had been slewed onto the course of the up main relief and down Windsor local lines. Rebuilding the side wall of the viaduct and filling the damaged Windsor line arches with rubble and ballast was not completed until December, with all eight lines becoming available again on Christmas Eve.

It was decided that the mail and newspaper trains should not return to Waterloo from their temporary suburban starting points. Wimbledon and Surbiton were kept as their departure stations until the end of 1941, because of the regular disruption from urgent danger warnings, as well as the possibility that the loaded trains might be stranded by bomb damage down the line. The volunteer siding platform at Wimbledon, which had road access for milk traffic, was pressed into use for the West of England newspaper train and the Alton line parcels train. Surbiton handled the trains for the Bournemouth line. Each evening the engine for the Dorchester mail arrived at platform 4 from Clapham Junction with the rolling stock both for the 22.30 departure for Dorchester and the 05.40 to Weymouth (both mail trains). Passengers for these trains reached Surbiton via the electric trains of the Portsmouth line. Earlier in the evening the vans arrived from Eastleigh and were shunted into the up sidings ready to form the 03.00 newspaper train to Bournemouth and Portsmouth. Its engine came down from Nine Elms later, following the empty mail trains. This was not an advertised passenger train, though it did include one coach, the existence of which soon became known to servicemen who often needed to travel at odd hours. With the stock for the mail and newspaper trains standing ready, should there be any damage to the line between Surbiton and the Nine Elms shed which prevented their locos coming down, three '*Lord Nelsons*' were kept fired up in readiness all night in Raynes Park goods yard, just in case they should be needed.

With air raids taking place every night, there was a reduction in London's evening social and entertainment scene, and consequently the railway could afford to reduce suburban trains into Waterloo after about 19.00 by operating shuttle services. These ran between Kingston and Shepperton, Leatherhead and Effingham Junction and Surbiton to Guildford via Cobham. As autumn came around and the nights grew dark progressively earlier many offices closed early and the rush hour began at about 16.00. This meant that there was now a greater requirement for trains around this time. The published timetables always seemed to be one step behind in keeping up with these train service changes.

A routine was soon developed for handling Waterloo's traffic in the face of almost nightly bomb damage. If the line was blocked between there and Clapham Junction, but Nine Elms locomotive depot was still accessible, then the main West of England and Bournemouth trains would start from Clapham Junction, but most of the Basingstoke-bound traffic would run to and from Woking. Suburban electrics would also run from Clapham Junction with Portsmouth and Alton trains starting from Wimbledon. If Wimbledon was the limit of operations, then all daytime steam trains would depart from Woking, leaving Wimbledon with only electric trains to deal with. On the Windsor line, the alternative terminus was Barnes.

On 26 September, Hinton Road bridge at Loughborough Junction was badly damaged, and almost as soon as single line working had been restored another bomb demolished the viaduct at the other end of the station, blocking the line for the remainder of 1940. On 27 September, in the early hours, enemy bombs fell to the west of Surbiton, near milepost 12.5 as well as between Earlsfield and Clapham Junction, derailing an empty electric train. As a result, Surbiton was at a standstill that morning and passenger traffic was routed via Wimbledon. On the way, at Raynes Park trains were halted by the congestion as they waited to get into Wimbledon, already busy with mail trains. From the exposed location of Raynes Park, passengers could see a formation of enemy bombers in the sky, but fortunately on that day at least they did not seem interested in inflicting more damage on the railway network. Over at Surbiton, just as repair work was being completed and trains were almost in apposition to resume service, a suspected delayed-action bomb was reported between the up and down through lines, causing the cessation of all movement until about midday on 28 September. By then, two trains of coal wagons had been positioned on the through lines to screen the bomb, thus enabling trains to use the local lines once again. The lines between Earlsfield and Clapham Junction had quickly been cleared and at Surbiton the bomb disposal teams dug down to a depth of 15 feet, finding nothing, and so came to the conclusion that the report was a false alarm. The coal wagons in consequence were removed on 2 October, and the through lines reopened to traffic. This enabled normal services to Waterloo to be resumed, indeed the traffic through Surbiton on this afternoon was extremely heavy due to the fact that everything had to pass by the bomb at walking pace on local lines. One of these, heading to Basingstoke was pulled by 'paddle box' No. 458 which two nights later was to become the only Southern loco to be lost to enemy action, when it was damaged beyond repair by bombing at Nine Elms loco depot.

On 9 October, a large bomb fell on the embankment west of Malden at 20.34, leaving a 40-foot crater across all four tracks. Portsmouth trains were diverted via Epsom and main line trains via Chertsey. The down local line was reopened for the passage of main line trains during the course of 11 October. That same day, an unexploded bomb was found in playing fields at Surbiton and a screen of wagons was placed on the down Hampton Court line, closing the branch for five days. Of greater concern was a delayed-action device which fell on Syon Lane during the evening, which when it landed buried itself 20 feet deep. The army believed that it might weigh as much as 2 tons, and so had evacuated a wide area before attempting with great caution to disarm it. Southern Railway was concerned about the impact of closing the important route to Feltham yard, but it would not be until 3 November that the army would allow freight trains only to pass on the line furthest from the bomb. Normal working on the Hounslow loop would not recommence until 29 November.

Back at Surbiton, at 06.50 on 10 October a delayed-action bomb did indeed suddenly explode nearby, damaging all five tracks and derailing the rear coach of the 05.53 from Guildford to Surbiton, fortunately no casualties were sustained. Four of the tracks had been repaired by the afternoon, releasing two engines which had been trapped at Surbiton by damage further down the line. There was more damage inflicted on the Windsor line the following night, when the Plough Lane underbridge at Clapham Junction was struck. One line was reopened on 14 October, but it would be the end of the month before all four roads here were operational once again.

Nine Elms goods depot was hit on 14 October and 'A' and 'B' sheds were severely damaged, but the blackest day for the South Western section of the Southern came on 15 October when shortly after midnight Clapham Junction 'A' signal box was damaged, leading to fears that it might collapse (this did in fact happen, but not until 1965!) Then, during the morning rush hour a daylight attack resulted in a bomb landing on arches A185 and A186 near Lambeth Road, killing six people below. The situation could have been much worse, as the bomb just missed the 08.15 from Shepperton which was then approaching the station.

The same day, Waterloo station was also hit. The destruction was not on the same scale as that at Charing Cross station a week earlier when a bomb had fallen on to the platforms at 08.48 just after a commuter train had arrived. Fortunately, in the case of Waterloo it was early evening when a bomb struck platforms 3 and 4, closing that side of the station for several days. One passenger on a Chessington train was injured but he had apparently ignored calls to take cover in the arches beneath the station where railway travellers – as well as hundreds of local people – took nightly shelter. The safety provided by these arches however was somewhat illusory. Some months later, two platforms at London Bridge would be hit by a bomb which penetrated the arch below and exploded, killing over sixty people sheltering there.

However, the worst incident on Southern Railway on 15 October came when a bomb demolished one of the 230-foot chimneys of the SR's Durnsford Road power station, wrecked one of the boiler houses and damaged the control room, injuring eight staff. All traction current was lost within the area between Egham, Esher and Epsom. Only the East Putney-Wimbledon line was still being supplied from Lots Road, and there were reports of electric rolling stock being pulled by steam tank engines, though how the brakes were applied without electricity remains unclear. By Herculean efforts, traction current was restored during the afternoon of 16 October, with the 20,000kw available from the undamaged portion of the power station being augmented by a further 6,000kw supplied via an emergency feeder from the eastern section. Power output was still only 40 per cent of normal so all trains within the suburban area were limited to 30mph, train heating was cut off and a number of peak hour services were cancelled. Normal output would not be restored at Durnsford Road until February 1941.

Trains resumed running into Waterloo on 17 October, though they were much delayed by wrong line working between Surbiton and Malden where a recently filled crater had subsided.

The next morning trains were again terminating at Wimbledon but by the evening the service was operating out of Waterloo once more. All was not well however, as Faulkner remembered:

> My train stopped for a long time outside Clapham Junction, where passengers were told to alight and join a large and rather impatient crowd waiting in the St John's Hill forecourt for a bus service to Wimbledon to be organised. This might not prove to be the familiar red London bus, but vehicles of many hues borrowed from the provinces to operate the numerous railway emergency services. I found later that a delayed action bomb had exploded in Clapham Cutting, blocking all tracks.[5]

With the clearance of the debris, the line was reopened on 19 October, just in time for the next visit of the Luftwaffe. This time a bomb was dropped on the through lines at Durnsford Road, overturning the last two coaches of a Waterloo to Hampton Court train, and resulting in one passenger killed and seven injured. Two sidings at Waterloo depot were blocked from 20 to 23 October, whilst on the evening of 22 October two pedestrians were injured when a bomb fell on the roadway from Lower Marsh and they fell through the crater into the sidings below. Several minor incidents followed – on 27 October four bombs fell near the Waterloo sub-station at 04.18, one of which blocked the main local lines and south carriage sidings. Then, on 29 October the roof of the old boiler house was damaged.

Nine Elms goods yard was also a regular target, as bombers could use the nearby river for guidance. Every attack resulted in considerable destruction of buildings, rolling stock and road vehicles, and on one occasion delivery carts were thrown on to the roof of the goods shed by the force of the blasts. One attack came on 16 November. Southern Railway like the others employed large numbers of women, and one of them was engaged looking after the horses in the company's stables at Nine Elms – not a

Nine Elms Goods Yard in London, seen just before the war. (Author's collection)

job for the faint hearted in 1940. (Southern Railway also had the distinction of employing the youngest signalwoman in the country, Miss Steel aged 22 who worked at the Old Shoreham bridge level crossing near Brighton.)

One of the most important locations on the entire Southern network was Feltham marshalling yard. An exchange as well as a shunting yard, it received traffic from the other railway companies through various junctions, sorted the wagons and sent them away by trains to stations on the south western side of the Southern Railway. Conversely it gathered up trains for other companies and sent them home. It also acted as an inter-sectional exchange for its own stations. It had 32 miles of sidings and handled roughly 6,000 wagons every 24 hours – 3,000 in and 3,000 out. Feltham was bombed by the Luftwaffe on at least 4 occasions but the worst attack was on 18 November 1940, when a landmine was dropped onto the down yard, causing major damage to the sidings and general office, wrecking 150 wagons and injuring 15 Southern Railway and other staff. However, tracks were re-laid and normal working resumed within a matter of a few days. The same day a delayed-action bomb near Sway caused the diversion of Bournemouth trains via Ringwood, a route with such severe weight restrictions that it forced the use of two pre-First World War engines until matters could be put right.

By now, the focus of the enemy was starting to shift away from the capital towards the suburbs and provinces. On 29 November, Luftwaffe activity over West Middlesex resulted in five incidents on Southern Railway property, including the demolition of the up side building at Sunbury station. Southampton experienced a heavy raid on the night of 30 November–1 December with four trains damaged, including a GWR No. 7308 on a Cheltenham train at Southampton Junction. Towards the end of the year, air raids and bombings seemed to happen every night, one raid wrecking a bridge at Woolston on the Southampton-Portsmouth line. Bill Bishop remembered:

> Next morning we were ordered out to clear the wreckage but the order was then cancelled before leaving the depot as they realised our crane jib was not long enough to reach the damaged girders. Fratton crew were then sent for and arrived at mid-day, but as it happened that day was chosen for a daylight raid and the crane presented a good target. Three of the crew took cover in one of the shelters from the nearby Supermarine aircraft factory but the crane driver had to make do as best he could under the crane. As it was, the shelter received a direct hit, killing all those inside, but the crane driver escaped without a scratch. It could have been us there at that time, we were very lucky.[6]

German bombers returned in force to the capital on the night of 8–9 December, when both high explosive and incendiary bombs hit the station at Hampton Court. In this raid seven electric coaches were burnt out and three other electric and three steam carriages were damaged. The main line rolling stock avoided damage as it was away from the station in the sidings. The same night a series of bombs fell between Waterloo and Vauxhall, with the most serious damage being sustained by arches 197–198 near the west crossings, blocking all tracks on the main line side. A limited electric service was established during the afternoon, using the Windsor lines into the terminus. The main line steam engines were diverted briefly to Victoria but the main through lines were reopened on the evening of 10 December.

In front of Waterloo a heavy bomb fell on the taxi exit roadway to York Road. The blast from this explosion almost destroyed the old LSWR general offices, but a more serious effect was the penetration of Waterloo and City tunnels far below the road, filling them with debris and 1.5 million gallons of water flowing from burst mains. Tackling this was at first delayed by the presence in the crater of what was thought to be a delayed-action bomb, but which later turned out to be merely a chimney cowl. It would prove necessary to completely rebuild the Waterloo and City tunnels and then restore the roadway, something that would not be achieved until well into the following year.

The end of 1940 was marked by the great fire raid on the City of London which took place on 29 December. This attack destroyed much of the Brighton-bound side of London Bridge station and whilst Waterloo was saved from the incendiary bombs which fell on its roof, damage was never the less done to tracks outside and to bridge 14 at West London Junction, where the up main through line crossed the West London extension from Latchmere Junction to Clapham Junction Central station. As a result both lines were closed until near the end of January 1941. Operations at Waterloo were brought to an abrupt halt by a British anti-aircraft shell which exploded prematurely after leaving the barrel, within an arch carrying signal and point cables from the power box to the platform. Linesmen from both London Transport and the army helped Southern Railway staff to piece together the thousands of severed wires and some platforms were back in use the following day.

The battered former general offices of LSWR at Waterloo sustained a direct hit at 21.36 on 5 January 1941, and what was left of the building was demolished in the incident. Prior to the war this building had housed the offices of the Southern Railway general manager and his deputy. Platform 21 was blocked by the resulting debris and the passageway to the Bakerloo tube was destroyed. Much of the LSWR paper archive was destroyed in this attack, a great loss for future rail historians. The ruins however were quickly cleared. Five days later on 10 January, Portsmouth Harbour station was badly damaged; the signal box was burnt out and bombs destroyed thirteen electric carriages. One coach fell through the decking into the mud beneath. The station was out of service until February 1941, but the signal box was not replaced until after the war. Eastleigh Carriage Works was the target on the evening of 19 January, and it was hit by several bombs. Five members of the first aid team were killed at their post, and one of the new five-car trains built for the Waterloo and City line was damaged.

February and March were periods of relative calm, in the London area at any rate, but major raids resumed once more on 16 and 19 April. At about 22.30 on the former date, the Necropolis station outside Waterloo was hit by high explosive and incendiary bombs which destroyed the building and wrecked the funeral train and other rolling stock at the platforms. Later, five separate bombs struck the viaduct between Waterloo and Nine Elms, and managed to block every track. At Waterloo the Waterloo and City line had no current for traction or for its pumps. A contractor had to bring in mobile pumps to hold back the inflow of ground water, while London Transport supplied enough power to run a reduced service. The main local lines were some 2 miles 3 chains from Waterloo on the steel viaduct alongside Nine Elms, so by concentrating work there it was possible to resume traffic into Waterloo the following afternoon, though with hand signalling and telephone block only between Waterloo and Loco Junction signal box. Later in the week, the Waterloo and City line had to be closed for two hours whilst the Royal Navy swept the Thames for mines dropped in this raid.

Charing Cross station however trumped all other localities for the severity of the damage which it sustained during this raid. Stationmaster Frederick Bassett, of Southern Railway, had been transferred to Charing Cross station in 1938. He received the MBE for his work here but he could not be publicly named until several months after the raid for security reasons; when details of the incident were published, the full story was revealed. During air attacks on 16 and 17 April Mr Bassett showed fine leadership and outstanding courage. His organisation of firefighting and rescue work materially assisted in minimising injury to personnel and damage to railway property. About a hundred incendiaries fell on the station and there were fires everywhere. Three trains were on fire, but fortunately the staff had a Coventry Climax fire pump ready and warmed up. By the light of flames from blazing rubble he discerned the faces of several railwaymen coming away from a bridge he was approaching. One of them, porter Gillett warned him to take care not to trip over the landmine – he thought this was an ill-judged joke until he discovered the mine resting against London Bridge signal box, its parachute still entangled in ironwork on Hungerford Bridge. He calmly gave orders to clear the area and then went over to ensure the signalman was safe. Later, he noticed fire coming from beneath platform 4. His own staff could not cope with any more work, and so Gillett volunteered to fetch help from the Westminster City Fire Brigade.

In the meantime, the fire was spreading, and approaching the landmine. Bassett remembered later that he had orders to evacuate the station, but his men refused to leave. Signalman Briggs, 67 years of age had stayed at his post in the signal box, adjacent to the mine, but now was told he was to leave. Eventually the fire brigade doused the flames, and a Royal Navy bomb disposal officer arrived to inspect the mine, which was made safe. Bassett recalled that the police were not wholly agreeable to his order to keep the road outside clear as well. They reminded him that the railways 'don't own the roads too,' but his wishes were obeyed – and proved right. This characteristic of 'sticking his neck out if he knew he was right' figured throughout his career on the railways. Whilst Charing Cross had miraculously avoided serious casualties, the same was not true at Southwark Street Bridge, where seven signalmen were taking shelter when a high explosive bomb destroyed the structure, and blew in the door of their shelter. Six of the seven died. Other awards, all BEMs went to John Edwards Smith, assistant lineman, Richard Henry Barclay, acting lineman of 53 Mayall Road, Lambeth, and to William Waller, station foreman, all of Southern Railway, for bravery in this incident. Barclay and Smith were both injured and Waller was severely shaken by the blast. Disregarding their injuries, however, they went to the aid of the casualties trapped in the shelter. Another man who was decorated here was Victor George Thomas Rickman, railway clerk, of Brooklyn Road, Bromley. Waller the station foreman and Rickman organised stretcher parties. In order to get the wounded to the street, Rickman led his party on a particularly hazardous journey across the badly damaged bridge. The rescue work was carried out in conditions of great danger, and all the men involved showed courage. The destruction of Southwark Street Bridge, together with the burning down of Blackfriars Junction signal box three nights earlier, caused severe difficulties for commuters into the city from the south.

Bombs had again fallen on Nine Elms locomotive depot. One landed on the fitters' shop and another hit the main shed; this one overturned two engines and killed two footplatemen who had taken refuge in the pit beneath No. 852 *Sir Walter Raleigh*. This engine was so severely damaged that it was not returned to service until June 1942. However, the depot had not been put out of action and a replacement engine quickly arrived for the Bournemouth newspaper train. On Saturday, 19 April, local electric trains were still terminating at Earlsfield, due to the earlier discovery of an unexploded bomb in the cutting at Clapham Junction. Main line steam services were still able to access the Windsor line platforms running via East Putney, but with long delays. This was in part due to a 15mph speed restriction due to another unexploded bomb, this time on top of the tunnel near

A memorial at Waterloo Station commemorating those killed by enemy action at Nine Elms. (Author's Collection)

Cromer Road signal box. Bomb disposal teams meanwhile could not locate the unexploded device at Clapham Junction, and so a screen of wagons was placed on the down through line to enable traffic on the local lines to resume from 15.15. The bomb was eventually found and removed on 24 April.

The main through lines at Nine Elms had reopened on 20 April but services were still restricted, due to damaged track circuits between Waterloo and Loco Junction. Damage to the viaduct on the Windsor line side was more serious, and it would not be until 3 May that a pair of tracks was reinstated, and 7 May before all four lines became available once more. Normal service was therefore restored just in time for the last and one of the most destructive raids of the London Blitz.

Between 18 and 20 April meanwhile the Luftwaffe had launched a sustained attack against the industrial centres of North Kent.

Southern Railway loco No 852 *Sir Walter Raleigh* seen before the war. (Author's Collection)

By the end, 71 people were dead, 500 homes were destroyed, 2,000 people were left homeless and 8 factories were destroyed, bombed into rubble and twisted steel. There was devastation in every corner of the region, from Sidcup to Bexleyheath and Crayford to Erith. Vickers, Thames Ammunition, Swaislands Printing Works and Alberts Products, in West Street, Erith, were destroyed in the firebombing. A direct hit hurled a train onto the platform at Belvedere station, the force ripping up 30 yards of track into the bargain. Stephen Robert Jeeves, a Southern Railway body maker's assistant, of Slade Green, Erith, gained the George Medal for leading an attempt to subdue fire enveloping trucks of exploding anti-aircraft shells. The citation read:

> A large number of incendiary bombs fell on a railway station and inspection sheds in which were six box wagons loaded with anti-aircraft shells and bombs. Two of the wagons caught alight, causing explosions in other wagons and the flying metal made the isolation of the blazing wagons dangerous.

> Jeeves led the attempt to subdue the blazing trucks of exploding shells. With two volunteers he ran forward with a hose but had gone only a few paces when one of the men fell fatally injured by a shell fragment. Jeeves carried on, but was eventually forced to give up because of the failure of the water supply. He then helped deal with the other fires.[7]

Jeeves went on to serve in the Royal Navy, and would lose his life in 1943 when the cruiser HMS *Welshman* was attacked by a U-boat.

On the Southern, passengers were disproportionately exposed to danger during the Battle for the Railways. Gladys Wilber was employed by the government in an office the Strand, and

Gladys Wilbur who travelled on the Southern Railway from Tunbridge at the height of the Blitz. (Author's Collection)

commuted from Tunbridge regularly through the early part of the war. She remembered:

> You didn't know if you would get home in the evening. We didn't close the office early, it was always half past five. Of course by the winter [of 1940] the blitz had started. I personally went to Charing Cross, and that was often closed, so then one went to Cannon Street, and that was often closed, then you went to Victoria, and if you were lucky, you could go and get a train from Victoria all the way round to Tunbridge Wells West station. That line was running, and I got home that way. The worst I ever did, was when I got home at half past eleven one night, that was the worst ever, my poor mother was nearly having hysterics. She was at the top of the road, she thought I was really done for that time, I was alright but it wasn't very nice. Of course in the train one was always … well [the Germans] made for the railway line, which wasn't funny, often I have been in carriages where the whole thing was [shaking] there were guns all along the railway line to defend them here and there, when they went off it was rather frightening …the trains were in black out, pitch dark, blinds down, little tiny lights in the ceiling but not enough to read by really. The blackout wasn't nice at all. Of course it didn't help when you were being bombed and everything's dark!
>
> We were machine gunned in the train once, that was nasty, one morning, that was in daylight, one of these lone planes came over, he came along and I heard a lot of sort of metal falling on the train. I thought, 'What on earth's that!' I poked my head out of the window, I was with a friend, there were only two of us in the carriage as trains were empty then, I said, 'Good gracious, it's a German machine gunning us!' There were always notices in the trains, if that happened you were supposed to lie on the floor, but it happened to be a wet morning, and of course we had clothes coupons but I thought,

> well I'm not going to lie on the floor in that muck! Anyway, we sort of got crouched down as far as we could, and he went the length of the train, and I said, 'oh good he's gone now,' but he turned and came back down the other side, but the driver was marvellous, fortunately we were near the Sevenoaks Tunnel, and he went into [the] tunnel and stayed there, full stop, and the Guard came along, and said is anybody hurt, I don't think anybody was hurt actually, it was very lucky, he must have been a rotten shot, and we stayed there for some time, and then we crawled out again. He'd gone off by that time.[8]

In fact, direct attacks on trains were not uncommon in this period. On 10 May 1941, a fine summer's evening, a Southern train was near Deal on its way from Ramsgate to Dover. Out of the blue, machine gun bullets rattled against the engine, as six German aircraft roared low above the train, deliberately aiming for the driver and fireman. The former, 50-year-old Percy John Goldsack was hit in the chest. His fireman, Charles Stickells was also hit. The two managed to halt the train and jump down on to the line, but Goldsack was mortally wounded and died shortly afterwards. Stickells tried to make it back along the train to the guard but fainted as he did so. The guard, Frederick Sabine had twice before been on trains that were attacked and in one of these instances the driver had also been killed. He was trained in first aid, and made a tourniquet for Stickells' arm, in which an artery had been severed, thereby saving his life. Luckily some Marines from the nearby barracks also came to the assistance of the train crew. They sent for a doctor, and notified Deal station of the situation. From here another engine was sent to connect to the rear of the crippled train. An order to use the 'wrong road' was obtained, and it was taken back to Walmer. Stickells eventually made a full recovery.

During the night of 10–11 May 1941 bombs fell on the north sidings at Waterloo, outside the station blocking the up main through and relief lines, close to Lambeth Road and near Vauxhall on the Windsor lines. Southern Railway driver Leslie

Cannon Street Bridge, a German intelligence photograph. (Public Domain)

Stainer of Lambeth was on duty on this occasion, and his report is a testament both to his bravery and his modesty. It reads:

> I booked on duty at 11.05pm and left the Loco Depot at 11.30pm to work the 12.53am Cannon Street to Dartford. On going up to Cannon Street between Surrey Canal Junction and London Bridge, a fire had started over by Surrey Docks and loads of incendiaries were dropped all the way to London Bridge and the City. We stopped the engine at Borough Market and the Fireman put out incendiaries. On arriving at Cannon Street, Platform 6, bombs began to drop, then the aspect signal lights all went out, and then some bombs dropped outside the station, bringing clouds of dust. A fire had then started at the side of the station, and it then rained bombs and there seemed to be no stopping. The fires were then like huge torches and there were thousands of sparks. The smoke from the fires blacked out the moon, and fires seemed to be everywhere, and then the station roof caught alight.

> To save the trains catching fire, two engines, coupled together, No. 934 and 1541, pulled out of Platform 8 onto the bridge. We stopped twenty yards ahead of the other train, and then, after about ten minutes we ducked down on the footplate. We counted three bombs, the last one was terrific, and very close. There was a terrific explosion and our engine seemed to roll; at first we thought our train had been hit. The debris flew in all directions – we were very lucky. My fireman said at the time, 'Look out, we are going in the drink,' and I said, 'I thought my back week had come.' We looked around, and found that the bomb had made a direct hit on the boiler of No. 934 engine, and it had also blasted our train, and turned part of the train over on its side.
>
> My fireman and myself went to see where the driver and fireman were, and I am pleased to say they had got off the engine in time. Then, looking round, we found our train had caught fire, and the fireman with buckets of water tried to put same out, but it was impossible as a strong wind was blowing up the Thames, and the fire got the master. I uncoupled my engine from the train, and drew back about two yards, and scoured the engine, and then crossed to the west of the bridge until dawn – watching the fires. It was just like as if Hell had been let loose. I am pleased to say there was no one injured and we were all lucky to be alive. Every railwayman at Cannon Street was very cool and calm, and all assisted in every possible way under those trying and unique conditions. That is my account of the Blitz.[9]

The driver and fireman of No. 934 had escaped death by a matter of seconds. They had climbed out of the engine on one side and were finding their way back to the station by the side of the train when the bomb dropped; in the smoke and confusion each shouted to the other to find out if he was alright. They took what cover they could find as they waited for the long hours of darkness to pass and for the raid to end. Two delayed-action bombs were also suspected in and around that station. As dawn broke on 11 May, Waterloo had no electric traction, signalling or lighting supply and with its feeder cables damaged the Waterloo and City line was also deprived of current. All train services were consequently terminated at Clapham Junction.

The worst damage however came from a bomb which had penetrated platforms 1 to 3 and exploded in the lower carriage roadway. Two fire watchers in the lost property arch lost their lives and the Southern Railway chairman's official motor car was destroyed. The explosion of this bomb started a fire in an arch occupied by a bonded warehouse and soon thousands of gallons of spirits were alight. As a result, soon afterwards the heat began to melt the asphalt of the platforms above. Firefighters were hampered by broken water mains and the blaze soon spread through the arch to the north side of the station. Gradually the fire burnt itself out and by the afternoon of 15 May it was extinguished. It was only then that the examination of the sub-structure of the station could commence. Track and ballast were then removed from platforms 4 and 5, in preparation for placing way beams across the damaged arch. In this task Southern Railway received help from the army, just as it had done following the Juxton Street bomb in September. It would be another five days before these platforms were reopened.

Meanwhile the numerous craters in the line had been repaired and suspected bombs had been dealt with. As a result, on 13 May electric trains on the main line side could run up to Vauxhall, continuing empty to reverse at the west crossings outside Waterloo. Windsor line trains were restored on 15 May which considerably shortened the replacement bus journey for passengers into Waterloo. Fast Portsmouth trains were diverted via Epsom to run to and from Victoria. After structural surveys were complete it was found that the portion of the arch carrying platforms 6 and 7 was safe, and there was a limited suburban service into Waterloo. The arches supporting the tracks into the remaining platforms had also been weakened and these too required strengthening with army assistance. Gradually, one by

A Home Guard stands watch over an unexploded bomb at Waterloo Station, September 1940. (Public Domain)

one the damaged platforms were reopened and full main line suburban services were restored from 22 May, with Windsor line services from 23 May and steam trains three days after that. However, it would be September before the damage to platforms 1 and 2 was made good and all twenty-one platforms at the station were fully operational once more. London's most bombed railway line was the 2.25 mile section between Waterloo and Queen's Road, Battersea. In the eight months of intensive bombing from September 1940 it had ninety-two incidents, the Railway Executive Committee later disclosed.

When war broke out, the management of Southern Railway had been the first to realise the necessity of maintaining telephone communications throughout the system, and avoiding the danger of dislocation by enemy action. This was particularly significant because after the war it was estimated that a third of the damage caused to British railways by the Luftwaffe was inflicted on Southern Railway. In the May 1941 attacks the telephone communication network was disrupted, as predicted, but the train service went on unrestricted. How this was accomplished was only revealed after the war, in an article in the *Kentish Express*. Fourteen emergency wireless stations were set up at various strategic points. Four of them were in Kent – Hothfield, Tunbridge, Orpington and Cuxton. In addition to these stations there were six mobile units always standing by. On the occasion referred to above the wireless stations came into operation immediately. Altogether some fifty-two operators and sixty-two coding clerks were engaged on this vital but secret work.

In the western part of Southern Railway, Southampton, Plymouth and Portsmouth had all been heavily bombed at the outset of the Luftwaffe campaign in 1940. Plymouth was also attacked again in April and May 1941. Richard Gordon Pinn, a porter signalman on the Southern Railway, was from Wadebridge but was stationed at Plymouth. During one particular raid a large number of high explosive and incendiary bombs fell on and around railway premises. A dray in a goods shed was set on fire. In the goods yard alongside there were several trucks containing ammunition, two of which were set alight, and the loaded shells exploded. Pinn, with help, hauled the dray to a hydrant and hose, and eventually extinguished the fire. Pinn showed great courage, with complete disregard for the danger presented by exploding

German aerial photo of the South Sidings at London Victoria station, Ebury Bridge in the foreground. (Public Domain)

ammunition, and by his prompt action valuable property was saved. He was awarded the British Empire Medal for his services. The most admirable aspect of these latest attacks on the towns of the south-west coast was the way in which the Southern and Great Western Railways helped each other. When Plymouth was bombed, the Great Western's main line traffic travelled to Cornwall on the Southern's line through Wadebridge, and did so again on 23 April when all communication between Plymouth and Devonport was cut. Five days later, Southern trains travelled over Great Western lines from Exeter. Each line came to the rescue of the other with unfailing readiness.

Meanwhile on the Underground the Waterloo and City line was at a standstill, flooded at Waterloo from the water being poured on to the fire above and with no power to drive its pumps. At the City end there were unexploded bombs in Queen Victoria Street and in Walbrook. The former exploded on 12 May and power supply was restored later that day, but removal of the Walbrook bomb in the busy heart of the city was a delicate task for the bomb disposal squad and it was not possible to reopen the 'drain' until 26 May. The worst of the 1940–1941 Blitz was now over, and the Southern Railway's third rail electrification had proved its worth. Almost as soon as the tracks were repaired on a damaged section, so traction current was restored, and the use of multiple unit trains enabled services to be turned around at any point where there was a crossover.

Because of its geographical location, Southern Railway suffered disproportionately at the hands of the German air service during the early part of the Second World War. In terms of overall size, it was the smallest of the 'Big Four', and yet it received more damage than any of the others, both in absolute terms and in terms of incidents per 100 miles of track. Furthermore some 170 of its employees were killed whilst on railway duty. It was none the less a testament to the skill and determination of its staff that it was able to continue functioning so effectively, in spite of the repeated heavy attacks and enormous damage that it sustained during this period.

EPILOGUE

Though the period of the Battle for the Railways demonstrated the great stoicism and courage under fire of the staff of the major rail networks, in many ways when they looked back and reflected, railway personnel felt that however nightmarish the experience was at times, it was not as bad as might have been expected. One of the things which had been anticipated and dreaded the most was the methodical and constant bombing of key points in the network, such as the Sutton Weaver Viaduct between Crewe and Warrington, which would have cut the direct route of LMS from the south and west to Liverpool, and to the North of England and Scotland. This would have in turn created a trail of disorganisation over large areas of the British railway system as a whole. Similarly, the junction at Northallerton, controlled by a single signal box, was the most vulnerable point on the whole LNER system. If that junction had been destroyed, the whole northeastern area with its network of vital lines would have been cut in half, but it was never attacked. It is also telling that, during this period, the total number of locomotives lost to enemy action by the major companies was only five. Hitler's principal aim seemed to be nothing more than causing havoc, without any sort of plan. The simplistic belief of the Nazi hierarchy was that aerial terrorism alone would be sufficient to bring Britain to the negotiating table, and end the war on their terms. However, their grave underestimation of the British people – and the British railway personnel in particular – possibly lost them the war; it certainly lost them the Battle for the Railways. It is perhaps fitting to close this epilogue with a poem written in 1940, at the height of the Blitz, by R.F. Thurtle. It is both apposite and moving:

Happy in peaceful service were our men
When the call came to some to leave awhile
The brake-stick, keying-hammer or the pen,
And take their stand within a martial file
They did not fail!

Flanders soon claimed them – seasoned men and young,
And proved their mettle on a testing ground;
In the red hells of Dunkirk, Calais and Boulogne,
Stern, valiant and unbroken were they found.
They did not fail!

England stands now, inviolate and at bay,
Alert and confident within her guarded coast,
And western men a worthy part will play
Through shambles be it or through holocaust.
They will not fail!

NOTES

Chapter One: London Midland Scottish at War

1. *London Daily News*, 1 October 1940
2. George C. Nash, *The LMS at War*, London, 1946, p.43
3. Op cit
4. Leonard Armitage recollections – author's collection
5. Alex Scott, *A Wartime Footplate Man*, Cromer, 2006, p.33
6. Nash, p.46
7. *Steam Days*, February–March 1991, p.37
8. Scott, p.30
9. *Carry On*, December 1941
10. *Liverpool Evening Express*, 13 March 1945
11. *Central Somerset Gazette*, 21 November 1941
12. www.bygonederbyshire.co.uk
13. *Daily Herald*, 9 July 1941

Chapter Two: London and North Eastern Railway Sees It Through

1. G.C. Potts, *Bankers and Pilots*, Truro, 1984, p.109
2. Charles Meacher, *LNER Footplate Memories*, Truro, ND, p.56
3. Reg Robertson, *Steaming Through the War Years*, Witney, 1996, p.45
4. Tom Quinn, *More Tales of the Old Railwaymen*, London, 2002, p.138
5. Norman Crump, *By Rail to Victory*, NL, 1947, p.50
6. *Bradford Observer*, 25 January 1941
7. *Yorkshire Post*, 25 January 1941

8. Gerard Fiennes, *I Tried to Run a Railway*, London, 1967, p.37
9. *The Scotsman*, 18 November 1940
10. halesworthmuseum.org
11. *Western Mail*, 15 November 1941
12. *Hull Daily Mail*, 15 November 1941
13. Crump, p.57
14. Crump, p.55
15. Crump, p.56
16. Tom Quinn, *Tales of the Old Railwaymen*, London, 1998, p.34
17. Op cit
18. Quinn, *Tales of the Old Railwaymen*, p.39
19. Geoffrey L. Raynor, *Geoff: 44 Years a Railwayman*, Warwick, 2000, p.35

Chapter Three: Great Western Railway Under Attack

1. *The London Gazette*, 8 August 1941
2. *Evening Dispatch*, Birmingham, 25 January 1941
3. Collie Knox, *The Unbeaten Track*, London, 1944, p.69
4. Knox, p.70
5. Quinn, *More Tales of the Old Railwaymen*, p.181
6. Op cit
7. Knox, p.172
8. *The London Gazette*, 28 March 1941
9. *Gloucester Citizen*, 29 March 1941
10. Op cit
11. Harold Gasson, *Firing Days – Reminiscences of a Great Western Fireman*, Oxford, 1973, p.17
12. A.W. Summers, *Engines Good and Bad*, Poole, 1985, p.30
13. Summers, p.33
14. Bill Morgan and Bette Meyrick, *Behind the Steam*, Bath, 1988, p.192
15. Knox, p.87
16. Knox, p.177
17. Knox, p.89
18. Op cit

19. Knox, p.79
20. *The London Gazette*, 24 January 1941
21. Knox, p.81
22. Jack Gardner, *Castles to Warships: On the Great Western Footplate*, London, 1986, p.74

Chapter Four: Southern Railway in the Firing Line

1. *Railways Southeast*, Winter 1990–1991, p.125
2. Railway Inspectors Reports, Ministry of Transport, 1940
3. Bill Bishop, *Off the Rails*, Southampton, 1985, p.21
4. *Birmingham Daily Gazette*, 11 January 1941
5. *Railways Southeast*, Winter 1990–1991, p.141
6. Bishop, p.22
7. *Jarvis Record*, 8 January 1942
8. Imperial War Museum, recording15969, author's transcript
9. Bernard Darwin, *War on the Line*, London, 1946, p.75

BIBLIOGRAPHY

Bishop, Bill, *Off the Rails*, Southampton, 1985

Crump, Norman, *By Rail to Victory: The story of the LNER in Wartime*, NL, 1947

Darwin, Bernard, *War on the Line: The story of the Southern Railway in Wartime*, London, 1946

Fiennes, Gerard, *I Tried to Run a Railway*, London, 1967

Gardner, Jack, *Castles to Warships: On the Great Western Footplate*, London, 1986

Gasson, Harold, *Firing Days: Reminiscences of a Great Western Fireman*, Oxford, 1973

Hooker, A.E., *Nine Elms Engineman*, Truro, 1984

Kingdom, A., *The Newton Abbot Blitz*, Oxford, 1979

Knox, Collie, *The Unbeaten Track*, London, 1944

McKillop, Norman, *The Lighted Flame: A History of the Associated Society of Locomotive Engineers and Firemen*, London, 1950

Meacher, Charles, *LNER Footplate Memories*, Truro, ND

Morgan, Bill and Meyrick, Bette, *Behind the Steam*, Bath, 1988

Nash, George C., *The LMS at War*, London, 1946

Potts, G.C., *Bankers and Pilots: Footplate Memories*, Truro, 1984

Quinn, Tom, *Tales of the Old Railwaymen*, London, 1998

Quinn, Tom, *More Tales of the Old Railwaymen*, London, 2002

Raynor, L. Geoffrey, *Geoff: 44 Years a Railwayman*, Warwick, 2000

Robertson, Reg, *Steaming Through the War Years*, Witney, 1996

Scott, Alex, *A Wartime Footplate Man*, Cromer, 2006

Summers, A.W., *Engines Good and Bad*, Poole, 1985

INDEX